Rethinking
Business to Business
Marketing

Rethinking Business to Business Marketing

PAUL SHERLOCK
Foreword by Tom Peters

THE FREE PRESS
A Division of Macmillan, Inc.
NEW YORK

Collier Macmillan Canada
TORONTO

Maxwell Macmillan International
NEW YORK OXFORD SINGAPORE SYDNEY

3-2-95

Copyright © 1991 by Paul Sherlock

The Free Press
A Division of Macmillan, Inc.
866 Third Avenue, New York, N.Y. 10022

Collier Macmillan Canada, Inc.
1200 Eglinton Avenue East
Suite 200
Don Mills, Ontario M3C 3N1

Printed in the United States of America

printing number
2 3 4 5 6 7 8 9 10

Library of Congress Cataloging-in-Publication Data

Sherlock, Paul
    Rethinking business to business marketing / Paul Sherlock;
foreword by Tom Peters.
        p. cm.
    ISBN 0-02-928615-8
    1. Industrial marketing—Management. 2. Entrepreneurship.
I. Title.
HF5415.13.S52 1991
658.8'02—dc20   90-43634
                                                            CIP

Dedication

To my three sons, Liam, John, and Jim, each a budding entrepreneur in his own way, who remind me each day of the roots of entrepreneurship—creativity, energy, and spirit of life.

Contents

PART THREE
Making It All Work

Foreword
by Tom Peters

I knew I liked Paul Sherlock's book when he put Velcro and Ziploc bags on his all-time best product list (they amaze you, he says), but left off personal computers (still a long way from being genuinely "user friendly," according to Sherlock). "Yes, yes, yes" I heard myself saying.

"Spirit," "dreams," goals that "stir the soul," "feeling the tempo" of the market, "getting the market culture into your bloodstream." And "relationships," "relationships plus magic," "intuition," "listening, listening, listening more," "integrity," "authenticity." These are a few of the surprising, and in engineer/psychologist/successful practitioner Paul Sherlock's hands, wonderful words that surface time and again in *Rethinking Business to Business Marketing*.

Technical product success is more about spirit and irrationality than analysis (by definition incapable of "creation," "breakthroughs," "profound insight") or rationality, "Hey, wait a minute," as football commentator John Madden might say. Is this book by some flake?

Hardly! Paul Sherlock, 16-year veteran of hardball marketing and product development at high-tech superstar Raychem and other entrepreneurial companies, provides detailed outlines for business plans and precise formats for market-information collection. He is as provocative while discussing—in great detail—how to cajole your way into a customer factory tour as he is when dissecting the irrational nature of customer decision making. Customers, high-tech or low, Sherlock writes, buy into—or don't—their "valuing image" of you. If you can make them "glow, tingle," you're OK. If you can't, you're in trouble. After the fact, of course, Sherlock observes, the buyer will construct a highly analytic and articulate rationale complete with factor weightings for his or her sophisticated purchase. But these analyses have virtually nothing to do with the real decision. Such rationales are a dime a dozen, or cheaper, and can readily justify the purchase of any non-awful product from any non-awful vendor.

This is a powerful book. Its breadth is stunning. Sherlock, with formal training in psychology as well as engineering and business, tells us on one page about the overarching importance of *authenticity* in both the selling and product-development process. A page later he gives practical but novel tips for choosing exactly the "right" restaurant for your *first* meal with a prospective new-product purchaser.

At times, Sherlock just plain surprises us (provokes us?). Regardless of the sophistication of the product—his experience is largely with the most sophisticated—he urges you to listen to "what your children say." If your child calls your pet idea "crazy," think about it, Sherlock counsels. Think about it a lot.

We are told in excrutiating detail about how to collect useful data from the market, how to pick the right journals to subscribe to—even how many issues to back order (about three years' worth). Then comes one of a host of surprising insights: calls are usually better than visits when trying to extract information from a would-be customer. (People have an odd tendency to tell you much more over the somewhat impersonal phone line than face to face, Sherlock tells us, with experience supported by psychological theory to back his claim.)

Then there are the utterly unique, to my experience, chapters that deal with distributor relations (courtship, marriage, maintenance, divorce), when and why to use or not use sale reps rather than a direct sales force, how to write compelling product literature (the entrepreneur/developer should always do the first draft, because only she or he has a true feel for the uniqueness of the product concept, the dream it represents), how to take advantage of trade shows (even how to most effectively staff your booth), how to give lectures that are memorable to would-be customers or industry gurus, how to place the right kind of article in the right trade journals in a timely fashion.

Sherlock is often contrarian, and always thoughtful. Raiding star employees from competitors is kosher, he argues, as long as you are bone honest about the job you are offering. Tough hombre, this Sherlock! But then he immediately adds that when *he* hears about a very exciting job that one of his key people might fill (perhaps with a competitor), he'll quickly tell the person about it and encourage him or her to take the job if it's more challenging than the person's current slot.

Rethinking Business to Business Marketing is practical and profound. It breaks new ground (marketing, selling, middleman relationships, product development, organization) and snickers at much of conventional wisdom. It is at once wildly challenging, deadly serious, and absurdly fun. Engineers will at times run for their lives from his psychological musings. But the psychologically inclined will run just as often from his hard-nosed demands.

When you finish, you will be confused. At least that's my hope. I suspect it's Paul Sherlock's too. You will have heard a lot that's practical—his descriptions and examples of Strategy Summary Statements (page 52) alone are worth the price of the book. You will have been challenged to your core.

Sherlock won't let you get away with an iota's worth of sloppy thinking, and he's the first to acknowledge that getting up an hour earlier than the competition is a must when you're trying to nudge a complex new product into the business market. But at the same time he encourages—even begs—you to dream, to honor your intuition, to view the world as the irrational, largely unknowable, wonder that it is.

Dig in and stand by to be challenged.

Acknowledgments

My interest in marketing started at the Harvard Business School as a result of taking an outstanding course taught by Professor Robert Davis (now of Stanford University). I have since had the opportunity to practice it with one of industry's most respected and effective technical sales forces, that of Raychem Corporation, during a period of tenfold growth. These experiences, and my subsequent new-venture opportunities, have significantly influenced my ideas.

Professor Henry Riggs also then of Stanford University enlisted me to teach Industrial Marketing and subsequently encouraged the writing of this book. Marilyn Kiernan transcribed my class lectures, which served as a basis for several of the chapters, with resourcefulness, skill, and humor; Emily Madriaga and JoAnn Scaduto typed the final draft. Thanks for the great job. Patricia Davidson, Patricia Lou, and Tom Dowling were very helpful with their skillful editing. I appreciate the encouragement, help, and critical reviews by Patricia Doss. Thanks to Phyllis Sherlock for her research and comments and to John Urquart for his review of the proofs.

Additionally, several friends and associates typed, read, or critiqued various sections. Each of you knows what you did; to each of you, my heartfelt thanks.

Introduction

I have often thought an introduction or preface is written either because the author is procrastinating rather than writing the actual book or is very worried that the reader will stray from the author's perspective. Despite this inhibiting notion, I find myself compelled to start with such wallowing—but promise to keep it brief.

This book expands two notions that may be quite different from traditional concepts of business-to-business marketing and sales. The first, detailed in Chapter 3, is that real choices (among those left over after the chaff is sifted out) are as unconsciously driven, as those relating to the impulse purchasing of consumer products, if not more so. The tortuous process called analysis becomes merely rationalization for the decision already unconsciously made. The works of psychoanalyst Carl Jung are drawn upon to provide background.

The second notion, detailed in Chapter 8, is a way of looking at the quality of selling that can be applied to all situations. It discusses three cumulative hierarchical levels as the ingredients of any salesperson's performance and describes what can be done and cannot be done to select and train for such performance.

The book is a short, easy to read "complete blueprint" of how to think about, plan, and implement the marketing and sales of your product. It should be particularly useful if you are among the following:

Actual or would-be entrepreneur. Follow the steps of each chapter and you will have your marketing plan complete and overall business plan outlined.

Experienced salesperson. You will have something against which you can test your experiences.

New sales, product management, or marketing support person. You will know what both you and your boss should be doing to-morrow.

Sales or marketing manager. It gives you a checklist for the many activities you are orchestrating.

Production, finance, or engineering person. It tells you how your marketing friends are enjoying the day.

Student. It will give you a ''down 'n' dirty'' description of the real world.

The chapters are followed by questions and suggestions intended to help you relate this information to your own personal interests. I think it is worthwhile for you to write answers based upon your pet product idea. By doing so, you will end up with a complete marketing plan.

Finally, in case you do not notice, the book is not objective. It is riddled with biases, heroes, villains, and buffoons. It is serious, satirical and, I hope, instructive. Throughout, however, is the unwavering theme that integrity and authenticity must prevail in the people, products, and plan if success is to be ongoing.

PART ONE

A New Point of View

CHAPTER

1

The Nature of Marketing

A surefire prelude to a boring speech is, "Let us start by defining the terms." I believe the same applies to writing, so
I will not start with a tortured, pompous definition of marketing.
In fact, even trying to think of one reminds me of a college sopho-
more trying to write a definition of life in Philosophy 1.

As you read the book, two realizations possibly will start creep-
ing over you. The first will be that "marketing is very easy." It
is easy and simple because this book describes marketing without
pretense, contrived concepts, mathematical formulae struggling
for relevant applications, and protective jargon. At the same time
it does offer much practical advice.

The second realization may be that "marketing is very difficult," because my version of it does not offer you a crutch of
jargon and formulae but rather taxes you as a person to the very
ultimate, where your energy, creativity, wisdom, intuitiveness,
ability to respond quickly and appropriately, resourcefulness,
and integrity must be at full throttle all the time.

With this little paradox as a starter, let us look at the process of
marketing.

The Marketing Process

"Once upon a time" all products started as the dream of some
entrepreneurially spirited person. This will continue to be so.

[3]

Such a spirit is the first element we will discuss in the marketing process. From the dream a goal is crafted, then the never-ending "swirl" or marketing process cycle begins. This cycle could be jumped into at any point, but at the heart of it all is an understanding of your customers and collectively the market. We might then list the steps around this cycle as follows:

1. Customer buys or potential customer is contacted
2. Finding out
      how the customer liked the product (if already on the market) or (if new idea) what is needed
      what is required to market the product
      what is happening with the overall market and competition
      what relevant resources in your company are available
3. Analyzing these data and creating a plan that includes
      goals
      strategy (the basic thrust) and its detailed ingredients (marketing mix)
         products
         sales people
         distributors
         product support/service
         literature
         advertising
         publicity
         trade shows
         seminars
      budget for the plan
4. Implementing the plan, which results in the *customer's buying the product* and includes
      organization
      implementation of the strategy and the marketing mix
      motivation
      coordination
5. Repeating the cycle starting with step 1 to make a better product sold with a better plan and continuously keeping this cycle going

While it is convenient to discuss the steps around the circle sequentially, usually they happen simultaneously. You are gather-

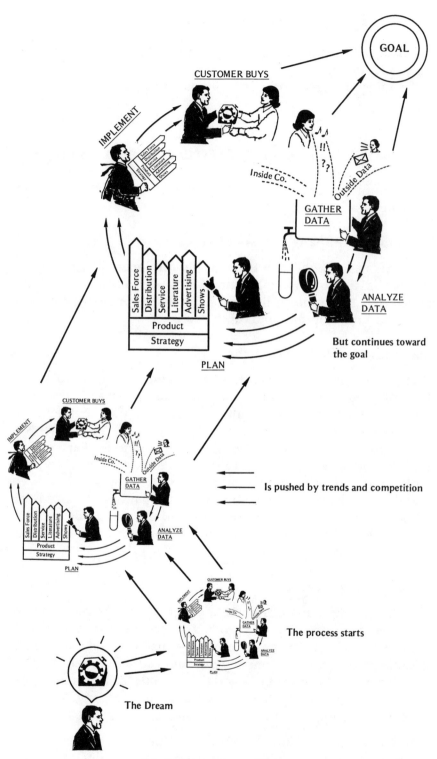

GOAL

CUSTOMER BUYS

IMPLEMENT

Sales Force
Distribution
Service
Literature
Advertising
Shows

Inside Co.

Outside Data

GATHER
DATA

ANALYZE
DATA

But continues toward
the goal

Sales Force
Distribution
Service
Literature
Advertising
Shows

Product

Strategy

PLAN

CUSTOMER BUYS

IMPLEMENT

Inside Co.

Outside Data

GATHER
DATA

Is pushed by trends and competition

ANALYZE
DATA

Sales Force
Distribution
Service
Literature
Advertising
Shows

Product

Strategy

PLAN

CUSTOMER BUYS

IMPLEMENT

GATHER
DATA

ANALYZE
DATA

The process starts

Sales Force
Distribution
Service
Literature
Advertising
Shows

Product

Strategy

PLAN

The Dream

Marketing Process Cycle

ing data while selling, analyzing and planning while gathering data, and so on.

We might represent this visually as shown on the preceding page.

Considerations to Clear Your Mind about Marketing

Before jumping into the marketing process cycle, let me submit some general thoughts.

The Entire Company Is Marketing

A company can only exist through the fulfillment of its customers' needs, and this is "marketing" in the broadest sense of the word. Hence, manufacturing is the "making" end of marketing, R&D the "developing" end, and so on.

Marketing Is "Nothing Special"

It is not a new language, nor a set of gymnastics, nor a script for a play. Rather it is simply a continuous exercise of alertness, assessment, and analytical thinking, intuition, judgment, and action—like much of the rest of life. Purveyors of "special tools" and jargon are often members of the marketing auxiliary which includes advertising agencies, public relations firms, consultants—and marketing book writers.

Stated another way: Marketing is understanding the needs of the situation—and the way resources and people can be applied to it—and then reacting appropriately, as opposed to following a formula.

Integrity Must Prevail

This is not simply moralism, but a congruity which must prevail throughout. Specifically, the product must be appropriate to the customer's needs, you must *believe* the customer will benefit by the sale, and that your company can fulfill *all* the responsibilities of the sale. All this must be in addition to your feeling thoroughly satisfied and proud of your working for your company. The reasons for integrity, in addition to the ethical issues, are simple:

- You cannot function at continuous high energy levels if you feel significant conflicts about what you are doing.

- The customer will sense any lack of congruity during the typically long period required to sell a business product.
- Customers have an exaggerated resentment if they are disillusioned.

However, integrity is not inconsistent with being strategic, strong, and determined.

Intuition: You Have It—Use It

We *all* have intuition, but we don't always trust ourselves to use it. Intuition is a far more powerful "management tool" than the best return-on-investment formula yet devised at the best of business schools. This does not mean avoiding quantitative analysis. In fact, rigorous analytical thought (or left-brain processing) serves to stimulate and focus the intuitive (or right-brain) activity. However, when your "sharp pencil" has become dull, put it aside and listen to your "gut feeling," to use that popular anatomical expression.

It is particularly interesting to consider that the two most important decisions that can be made in the entire business spectrum *must* be made based upon intuitive assessments. These decisions are:

- What product or market direction to choose when the quantitative analysis shows two or more alternatives to provide approximately the same opportunity.
- How to select and place your people.

Professionalism Yes, but Professionalism May Not Be What You Think It Is

Our society has given professionalism connotations of rigidity, dress codes, restraint, manipulation, coldness, impersonal and pompous behavior (including gesturing with glasses while haughtily sniveling).

Professionalism's true meaning is integrity, open-mindedness, enthusiasm, profound depth of knowledge, and a sincere interest in your customers and associates as people, not gears in an organizational mechanism.

No One Can Create a Company Image

The image is the sole creation and property of the customer. The notion that you can create your image is the self-serving pomposity of advertising and public relations flacks. The best you can do as a company offering a product is to create and furnish substance and igniters. *Substance* is a product or service of real quality, appropriate to the buyer's need. *Igniters* are triggers to unleash the most favorable image in the customer's mind and are in the literature, advertising, presence of the salesperson, and all other elements of communication.

A product of substance with no image igniters is a bore and will not sell. Good image igniters with insufficient product to back them up are a fraud, doomed to fail in the long run. A product of adequate substance with exaggerated or inappropriate igniters will eventually disillusion a customer. The meaning and detail of this concept of igniters will become clearer as you read the later chapters.

Living with That We Cannot Understand

Since I naturally think this book provides a dimension absent in prior books on marketing and have drawn upon some of our leading psychologists to describe behavior in the buying process, I must quickly admit we cannot truly *understand* buying decisions. To do so would be to reach the very essence of human nature and this is not possible.

To start with, we cannot *really* understand ourselves. For example, we cannot really explain why we are with our present employer (other than that IBM hired us out of engineering school and we left after five years for the chance to get a piece of the action elsewhere); nor do we know why our company is making disc drives (other than that Peter Spinoffe, the president, once also worked for IBM and seems to be quite taken by disc drives).

Similarly, we cannot *really* understand our customers, and why they *really* make the choices they do. Granted we all know that price, reliability, service, support, product performance, size, weight, and a multitude of other "perceived product benefits" are important. And we understand that our firm's good reputation, our customer's nasty "politics," and the buyer's personal need to minimize risks are all factors.

But what are the deeper factors? There certainly must be some because in any competitive situation, perceived "customer benefits" can be seen different ways. Otherwise there would be no competition and only one supplier! Stated another way, why is one set of apparent "facts" interpreted one way one time and another way another time, even by the same customer? We will never be able to explain this at its root. The intention of this book is to provide a new, different, and perhaps provocative view of this buying behavior.

Between our own and the customer's unfathomable regions is that layer of awareness, consciousness, and willpower that we can utilize and control. Within this area we can assess a situation, plan a strategy, and carry it out in a way that allows our unconscious, with its wisdom and bumblings, and our customer's equally mysterious and unconscious responses to create the best prospects for a sale. This may be another way of describing the *process* of marketing.

The purpose of the following chapter is to lobby a point of view; namely, the importance of the entrepreneurial spirit, and the all-important starting point, the entrepreneur's dream and the translation of this into a do-able goal. From there the book carries you step by step around the marketing process cycle—starting with that vital point, the customer's decision to buy.

2

The Spirit and Dream of the Entrepreneur

Are you in earnest? seize this very minute—
What you can do or dream you can begin it,
Boldness has genius, power, and magic in it.
Only engage, and then the mind grows heated.
Begin it, and the work will be completed!

—Goethe[1]

In this chapter we will discuss the nature of entrepreneurship. Let me state immediately that entrepreneurship is a state of mind and not necessarily a description of the struggling, starving genius trying to start a business. You can work for a well established company such as 3M or DuPont and still have an entrepreneurial spirit. The key message here is that marketing carried out by people with entrepreneurial spirit can result in a multifold return compared to what can be done by bureaucrats.

What Is the Entrepreneurial Spirit?

Entrepreneurship is best seen in the results achieved. It is changing rather than maintaining "landscape." It is the successful in-

[1]Johann Wolfgang von Goethe, *Faust: Vorspiel auf dem Theater*, 1. 227 (1806), as translated by John Anster, *Faustus, A Dramatic Mystery: Prelude at the Theatre*, 1. 303 (1835).

troduction and growth of a new product. It is the breathing of new life into an old product—creating an upsurge in its existing market or discovering a new one. It is the creative matching of a technology with a market in a way that others have not seen. It is successfully acting on the perception that a demand can be created. It is sensing and reacting when a "window is opening" in a marketplace. A comparison of the entrepreneur with the bureaucrat may clarify the concept.

How They Think

The Entrepreneur	The Bureaucrat
• Knows and "feels" the market—its tempo, sound, smell, and the people who influence it.	• Authorizes a market research study.
• Knows with unshakable faith the product is right for the market.	• Does cost effectiveness and comparative competitive studies.
• Makes commitments, *then* figures out how to do it—intuitively knowing it can be done.	• Commissions a feasibility study.
• Is "driven"—the endeavor seems to infuse inexhaustible energy.	• May even like the work.
• Functions on "if it works, use it."	• Wants a properties characterization report.
• Is singularly dedicated—everything revolves around this venture.	• Devotes appropriate time to it.
• Mentally asks "How can this enhance the venture?" of everything seen and done.	• Doesn't ask.
• Gets "free" moonlighting work from other departments or friends as a result of contagious enthusiasm.	• Is upset that the new department budget is not approved yet.

How They Act

At the Factory

The Entrepreneur	The Bureaucrat
• Starts work at 7:30 A.M.	• Starts at 8:30.
• Makes key phone calls or sketches some new ideas.	• Has coffee.
• Goes to the lab.	• Phones the comptroller.
• Carefully examines the samples to be sent to the customer.	• Tells secretary to send the samples.
• Goes over to talk with the technician about yesterday's tests.	• Phones for a status report.

On a Trip

The Entrepreneur	The Bureaucrat
• *Makes first appointment at 8:00 A.M.*	• Says people need time to clear their desks. Calls at 9:00 A.M.
• Makes second call at 9:30.	• Breaks for lunch at 11:15.
• Takes third customer to lunch.	• Uses lunch to review accounts with the local salesperson.
• Starts afternoon calls at 1:30 P.M.	• Makes first appointment at 2:30 P.M.
• Meets former employee of competitor for interview dinner.	• Meets old classmate for dinner.
• Flies to next city later that night.	• Goes to bed and leaves on the 8:30 A.M. flight the next morning.

This comparison could go on and on, as the spirit of entrepreneurship is in the region of magic, not quantifiable science. However, the final test of entrepreneurship *is* quantifiable. Is the venture successful?

Most of Us Are a Combination

All entrepreneurship and no bureaucracy would result in chaos. Fortunately, most of us have some elements of both traits. A little

bureaucracy (but not too much) results in some semblance of order, planning, budget control, and general tidiness. *Know when to
use which.*

The Entrepreneur Versus the Creative Gadfly

Successful entrepreneurship is distinguished by the program's
being "do-able" (the match between the technical idea and a
market need is viable) and by the entrepreneur's sticking with
the program at least until success starts to "roll." This requires a
special kind of person who combines the creative and energetic
spirit previously described with a significant dose of wisdom,
groundedness, and self-discipline. For every person like this
there may be several creative gadflies who are incorrectly perceived to be entrepreneurs. I am sure each of us can recall several
we know. They are always starting new ventures. The ventures
are purely the products of their imaginations and usually not acceptable in the marketplace. Even if they were, we would never
know because the gadflies are off to the next project before their
current one really gets started. These people can be very useful
as idea spigots, but they are not responsible entrepreneurial managers.

Three Final Cautions

First, as a successful entrepreneurial marketing manager, singularly driven, whose entire life revolves around your venture, always remember that you are *doing* something, not necessarily
that you *are* that venture. Find time to "smell the roses," play
with the children, do something that is totally foolish, and laugh
at your venture. You will be a better entrepreneur for it.

Second, entrepreneuring does not mean going hell-bent for
whatever, and the consequences be damned. Our world is too
crowded, complex, and tenuous for that. The mature entrepreneur first assesses the social, ethical, environmental, and economic effects of the venture, and then continues to be aware of
them as he assumes responsibility for these consequences.

Third, the entrepreneurial spirit describes the energetic and
achieving way such people go about doing things with the traits

and skills they have. The entrepreneur cannot necessarily be all things to all people. Thus, the successful entrepreneur teams up with others who demonstrate the same spirit, but have *complementary* traits and skills. This can be difficult because we often prefer to associate with those people who reflect our own image.

The Dream and, from It, a Goal

Triggering any entrepreneurial venture is the dream: a vision of the new plant, designed to be harmonious with the rolling landscape, the product in its rich blue-grey housing, manipulating its digits three times faster than the nearest competition and being praised in all the trade journals of the world, 539 happy employees arriving at work one half hour early for the pure joy of creating, your own red Ferrari parked nearest the entrance, not because you have marked spaces in your democratic operation, but because you have arrived at 5:00 A.M. to test your next new idea for a whole new generation of giga-digiters. Meanwhile, profits are pouring in and the investment bankers are clamoring to take another issue public.

Before we start into the marketing process cycle we must convert this dream into a goal—so let us discuss goals for a moment.

There are two origins of goals: the first from an inner vision, and the second from a cultural code (such as a boss who has been to a course on management by objectives—MBO). A goal that originates internally is alive, filled with passion and inspiration—our vision of the future which we strive to fulfill. A goal imposed by external forces is boring, burdensome, and rarely thought of after the torturous task of writing it down is finished. The first kind of goal is an expression of creativity, perhaps brought to life by the hero archetype. The second kind is the product of our culture, which says you are not worth much if you don't get an A in the course and even less if you don't have a goal to do so.

The visionary goal can be wrong. The powerful inspiration can be about the wrong product, the wrong plan, or at the wrong time. Because it is a product of the crusader's inner energies, objective assessment is often inadequately done or not listened to. On the other hand, the "mechanically" arrived at goals, by their nature, get much more objective scrutiny. But they will not work unless they have an ingredient of inspiration or passion, because the effort will lack energy.

While I think it is *possible* for a person simply to exist without a goal and still live with such excellence and quality that success is an assured by-product, our culture does not work that way. Most of us feel uncomfortable without goals. In a company where goals are ambivalent or not clearly stated the people are often frustrated. So, until we all reach a higher plane of functioning we are stuck with goals—but they had better be ones that contain an ingredient of inspiration.

Goals may be honed, changed, or even abandoned as a result of logical processes, but beneath it all the goal is based simply upon the nature of the person setting it. For example, as a result of a perceived market trend the founder of a semiconductor company alters the goal of being a leader in specialty bipolar devices to one of leadership in CMOS technology. This is a logical refinement of a goal. However, the founder's being in the semiconductor business in the first place is simply the result of that person's nature.

Having a dream and from it extracting a goal applies to situations other than just the entrepreneurial start-up. It can be that of a product manager in a large company introducing a new product, a market manager trying to increase significantly sales of existing products for next year, or a salesperson opening a new territory.

Extracting a Goal

First the dream must pass the test of having the four following ingredients.

1. *Sufficiently large market.* The total market for the specific product must be significantly larger than your company forecast. (Details of market assessment and forecasting are in Chapters 4 and 5.) How much more of course depends on the situation, but even in the best of worlds, where the product is first on the market and highly proprietary, it should be 2:1. On the other hand, if there are many competitors and a more mature market, 10:1 is a better benchmark.

2. *A valid reason for being.* A goal must be more than simpl̖ desire to be in the field. Your product must be better, you must have a strong sales force that needs the product to fill out the line, or your costs must be lower, or you must be first on the market (or second, with something the first company did not have).

3. *More than sufficient capability,* including adequacy of re- sources. This starts with having the intelligence, maturity, and presence to attract the additional talent and money ad- equate for the endeavor. It does not mean having all the people and money to start with, but rather the power to bring them in as needed.

4. *Pure passion by the people doing it.* The dream must be soul stirring, not an idle fantasy, and must pass these quantify- ing hurdles with passion intact. The leader must feel it so intensely, and be able to communicate it so infectiously, that every member of the group possesses it. Without this shared passion, the endeavor is bureaucratic, not entrepre- neurial.

Once these ingredients are present the goal can be drafted. It will be refined later after the market is fully understood. The goal statement should be both quantitative (product definition, posi- tion in the market, sales and profit goals for five years, return on investment) and qualitative (values and principles of doing business).

Your Plan

1. We all do best when we are working from our strengths. Of all your characteristics or traits, which ones would serve you best as an en- trepreneur getting a product on its way?

2. None of us can be all things to all people, yet a successful venture needs a balance of traits. Typically we would bring in one or more partners to round out our flat sides. What specific traits would you look for in a partner? Consider skills and knowledge as well as per- sonality traits.

3. Write your entrepreneurial dream in some detail. Be poetic if you wish, sketch, if you are so inspired; do not worry about order or format, but be sure to include a description of the product, the cus- tomers, your plant, your people, how you want to be seen, what

you want out of it, and your values regarding the product, customers, and your employees.
4. Realizing you have not gathered market data yet, try to answer the
   four test of viability questions.
   a. Is the potential market sufficiently large?
   b. What is the valid reason for the product's being?
   c. Do you have more than sufficient capability to do the ven-
      ture, or if not, to acquire the sufficient resources to do it?
   d. Do you and your team share a pure unadulterated passion
      for the product and the program?
5. If the answer is yes to all of these, fill out your statement of a goal.

My goal is to create _____

_____

occupying _____ position in the market with sales

in five years of $_____, profit before tax of _____%, and return on

investment of _____%. The company will operate with the following

values: _____

_____

3

The Irrationality of "Rational" Buying Decisions

The Commonly Held View of Business Buying

When we talk about the "buying decision" we mean not just the purchasing agent's decision to write the order, but even more important, the design engineer's decision to incorporate the product, the reliability engineer's approval of the product, or the manufacturing department's adoption of it. In other words, all that is written in this chapter applies to any of the customer's decision levels.

Before we can usefully examine selling and its larger framework, the overall marketing job, we must try to understand what goes on in the throes of decision making. Let us start by examining some assumptions and typical attitudes toward the business product buying decision. If we were to ask customers how decisions are made in their organizations we might hear the following replies:

- "It's performance that counts."
- "We're objective. We make a thorough analysis and pick the highest-ranked product."
- "Consumer buying is very emotional, but industrial buying is a hard-headed, calculated process."

- "Our engineers do a thorough technical comparison. Purchasing evaluates vendor performance. We consider all these factors and make an objective decision."

If a decision seems to defy this logical description and goes against us, we usually describe it as "political," or say "the competition had them in their pocket."

Instruction for the technical selling encounter (if any is included in the sales training) is devoted to teaching how to sell "logical benefits" that the customers should of course immediately embrace. (And if they do not, then how to probe for hidden "objections" that, once dragged to the surface, can be devastated with a barrage of logic.)

What Really Happens

Such notions are simply perpetuations of the cultural myth that business is rational; particularly, engineers in business are rational. In reality, an entirely different mechanism prevails, one that is not logical or rational but perhaps more wise, and certainly awesome.

To realize this you need only look at some of your own experiences. Let us consider some typical situations, starting with a homey example. You are in the market for a house and the second one you visit "grabs you." You continue looking (after all, you need some basis of comparison to make a sensible decision), and find some that meet certain of your needs better. One is closer to the school, another is in better condition, and a third seems to be more for the money. The "more for the money" one seems like the one you *should* buy since it is also close to the school, but you cannot get that second one you saw out of your mind. You think about it for a few days and conclude that with the rising price of real estate "best buy" means little, that some extra exercise in getting to school is good for the kids, and doing repairs is a good hobby to develop. Therefore it makes the most sense that you buy that second house.

Now you have moved into the house, and in your job as an engineer at Devastation International Aerospace Inc. you must choose between two servo motors for an aircraft subassembly. Approaching the decision logically, you have listed everything you know about each, as follows:

Cost	$14,850	$15,195
Weight	4.5 lbs.	4.0 lbs.
Size	80 cu. in.	68 cu. in. (but has long actuator shaft that might be in the way)
Life expectancy	10,000 hrs.	12,000 hrs.
Overload capability	160%	150%
Environmental capabilities	−70° to 200°	−65° to 180°
Reputation of company	old-line, conservative, reliable	aggressive, innovative, tries harder
Service to date	excellent	tries harder
Product experience	never used either company's product	
Sales representative	knowledgeable but distasteful	entertaining but technically dumb
Delivery (12 weeks needed)	18 weeks	14 weeks

How do you "logically" approach this, since either product would work? Ah, simple. You may say "First, just array the factors in order of importance." But is cost more important than size? Just how much is size worth? You can give a value to weight in terms of fuel savings, but over what life of the product and at what fuel price? Once you have them arrayed, how do you factor them? Is cost twice as important as size? For a value factor, is a 10% reduction in size weighted 1/10 or is it so important that it should be multiplied by a scaling factor? If so, should this be linear, logarithmic, or something else?

If you think this is a simple decision, imagine trying to follow this procedure in comparing two similar computer installations or in choosing between a Boeing 767 or an Airbus A310 for an airline.

As must be obvious by now, your mind is boggled. Computer analysis does not help because you must make all the important decisions before feeding them in: the array of the variables, the weight given each, the weighting factor given the variation of each variable.

You go home, have dinner, watch television with a beer, and go to bed—still mulling the decision over in your mind. The next morning it all seems clear—weight is all that really matters, since this is a high-performance plane. You write your justification, and the boss likes it.

Now let us look at a few more situations that are certainly familiar to any experienced business person.

- One of your longest-term customers suddenly starts buying 30% of its needs from an adequate but unimpressive competitor. To make matters worse, the competitor's salesperson is only two years out of college.
- An engineer of one of your customers becomes so enthusiastic about your products that he literally becomes an inside salesperson. You cannot understand what is driving him.
- An evaluation seems to be going nicely, but suddenly you are rejected for unclear reasons. Furthermore, the key decision maker becomes unfriendly, virtually overnight.
- In case studies in business schools or executive training programs, two equally capable people present equally well-reasoned positions for quite different solutions.

I will offer some explanations of these examples, but first let us look at some general conclusions about buying decisions and some background psychology.

What Can We Conclude Thus Far?

Based upon these few examples and others we can draw from our experiences, I suggest the following:

- The human mind simply cannot, even with the aid of a computer, array and weigh the factors in a complex decision with the so-called "objectivity" we like to think possible.
- Struggling with these factors in an "objective" and analytical way, however, does accomplish two things.
  - First, it may narrow down the decision. Some alternatives may be properly rejected by analytical observation.
  - Second, the mere process of struggling and groping with the "facts" in the conscious mind seems to unleash another force which comes to the rescue before burnout or terminal uncertainty sets in. This force functions in much the same manner as weeping and laughter do, the first rescuing us from acute grief, the second from incomprehensi-

ble incongruity. Suddenly we start feeling what is important and the decision becomes more obvious.

- Arranging the "facts" to form a justification for this decision is relatively easy. We saw earlier that we cannot array and weigh factors objectively to reach a decision. However, *after* the decision is made we can easily array and weight the factors to support it. This is a surprisingly simple process, since the issues are so complex and numerous that it is very convenient to select and develop the factors to support most any reasonable choice.

- Everything we see, every person we meet, can trigger a flood of associations and feelings. These are based on previous experiences and are simply associated with the immediate situation due to some thread of connection. Such floods of imagery occur when we are faced with a buying decision, giving us a positive or negative tilt toward the decision. With consumer products we usually respond to this instantaneously, either by buying or not buying on the spot. We feel comfortable saying "I bought it because I liked it." No further justification is needed.

- In business buying, the culture demands analysis and justification. Thus this initial tilt has to be repressed until the struggle with the "facts" reaches its point of no return and that inner feeling emerges to provide the answer. Usually this conclusion is simply the earlier "tilt" coming back at an acceptable time. Stated another way, the decision is made at the very beginning, denied because of the cultural need to analyze, keeps pushing unconsciously to convert our analysis into a rationalization until, when the rationalization is sufficiently aligned with the earlier tilt, a recognized conscious decision emerges. A formal, i.e., written, rationalization (the analysis and justification) soon follows.

Now, to provide these conclusions with some background, let us look at some psychological theory.

The Nature of the Mind

Carl Jung, the eminent Swiss psychoanalyst, identified three regions of the mind: the conscious, the personal unconscious, and the collective unconscious with its archetypes.

The Conscious. This is the area in which we "think" we function. It contains our willpower, our logical thinking ability, and our immediately accessible memory. It is one of the truly distinguishing aspects of the human species and must be cherished, expanded, and nurtured to better control our lives. It is, however, a boat rocking on the vast sea of the unconscious with its two levels.

The Personal Unconscious. This is the region of our forgotten personal experience. Everything we have ever seen, done, or felt is stored there. Some experiences float back and forth into consciousness (we remember, then we forget). Some are so deep only the effects will surface, such as when we feel a certain emotion or have some images we do not understand upon seeing someone again or something new for the first time. We may say, "That person reminds me of someone . . ." Our likes and dislikes stem from this region, patterned on long-forgotten positive or negative experiences.

The Collective Unconscious. While this theory has been debated by psychologists, particularly behaviorists, I believe it is strongly applicable to human behavior, specifically the function of decision making.

This concept is that human beings are more than just programmable mechanisms, responding only to the environment; rather we are born with an inherent nature, and our minds contain primordial "archetypes" or themes that are universal to all humankind. Some of these themes are mother, father, the playful child, the journey of the hero, propensities for creativity and power, transformation, wisdom, happiness, the spiritual, the trickster, and the shadow.

These themes, among an undetermined number of others, are predispositions in the way we react to the world or, as Jung stated, "contents and modes of behavior that are more or less the same everywhere and in all individuals. The collective unconscious . . . thus constitutes a common substrate of a suprapersonal nature which is present in every one of us."[1]

Evidence for the collective unconscious and its universal themes can be seen in the art, literature, folklore, dreams, and mythology of many cultures from many ages. While Jung articulated the concept more extensively than anyone else, others—

[1]C. G. Jung, *The Archetypes and the Collective Unconscious,* Vol. 9 of *The Collected Works of C. G. Jung* (Princeton: Princeton University Press, 1959), Part 1, p. 3.

among them Plato, Kant, Shelley, Blake, and Whitman—have suggested this basic concept.

The themes are universal, but the specific content is personal. For example, the archetype of the hero's journey may be seen in these forms:

- The brave youth slaying the dragon in Greek myths or medieval romance.
- The stock car driver in South Carolina.
- The beer-drinking slob bursting out of his T-shirt as he gapes at his TV, identifying with the washboard stomached football heroes.
- The engineer who is "staking his reputation" on your innovative servo motor design—the one who has become the "inside salesperson" mentioned earlier.

The emotions connected to these basic themes are extraordinarily powerful, and the more the person is in the grip of the archetype, the more powerful they are. Yet the archetypical source is not recognized at the time. It's like being instantly, madly in love with someone you hardly know; an example of the "opposite sex archetype." Here the other person serves to trigger the energy and power of this theme in your deepest unconscious. Later, perhaps, your conscious level will discover whether or not there is a suitable partner there.

A response may also come from an inappropriate archetype. The buyer in my earlier example who switched from a long-term supplier to a new firm represented by a young salesman might have been overcome by his father archetype. Possibly the buyer's unresolved feelings about his own father, who was a poor masculine role model, have caused him to attempt to "replay" his father's role with the projected "son." The aggressive "inside salesman," whose motivation seems unexplainable, might be in the throes of a hero journey. And in the situation where you were rejected without warning, the customer might have suddenly projected the shadow archetype upon you, for some behavior of which you were totally unaware. The shadow, in Jungian terms, is the region that includes each person's least developed, most unconscious, and often destructive capability. Prejudice and unfounded hatred may stem from this archetype. Every day, in the world situation as well as in personal relationships, we see people hating and accusing those they do not even know. This can happen in the sales situation where the salesperson's appearance, dress, or words can trigger inappropriate negative reactions.

The product itself, rather than the salesperson, can unleash archetypes. For example, executive jets may touch several deep themes, including those of power, the hero, and the playful child. (There has to be something very powerful involved to support the "rational" structure necessary to purchase a $10 million toy.)

The deep, powerful themes of the archetypes are not tapped in all cases. In the example of buying the house, possibly only some early experiences stored in your personal unconscious tilted the decision. Likewise, the decision on the servo motor may have gone no deeper than hearing "weight–high performance" enough times from the right people. On the other hand, if the emotions about it were very strong, the hero archetype (jetting into the wild blue yonder) may have been involved.

Reconciliation of the Unconscious with the "Logical"

Now the decision process I have just described is quite contradictory to what the popular view holds, or even what training in decision making teaches. The popular view was touched upon in the beginning of the chapter, and goes something like this: establish criteria, gather the data, analyze the data against the criteria, pick the most logical alternative.

How do we reconcile this popular view and the actual unconscious-driven process? By what was mentioned earlier, a *post-decision analysis* or *after-the-fact rationalization*, which is not acknowledged as such, of course, but really is just that. As an example, listen to the two following justifications:

Company A: "We chose IBM personal computers because of the reputation and service of the company. We know they will be here tomorrow to support us. The equipment may not have had quite the performance of some of the newer units, but it was right there in the ballpark."

Company B: "We chose Rutabaga computers because they had the greatest processing capability of any yet developed. This technology is moving so fast you have to get the most advanced or be left behind. The company is only five years old, but has an outstanding record."

Either is a plausible rationale, and would probably satisfy the decision maker's boss. They are examples of two companies utilizing two different sets of selected factors from the same body of data, which actually contains dozens or hundreds of such factors. In each case the subconscious activity tipped the decision (likely the mother archetype in Company A and the hero archetype in Company B), and the appropriate and "logical" sets of factors were assembled so both the decision maker and boss could feel comfortable—pretending a "rational" decision had been made. Incidentally, as will be discussed in detail later, the good salesperson assists the buyer in this after-the-unconscious-decision rationalization.

Additional Considerations

It is important that a couple of factors be emphasized.

First, everyone's psyche is of the same general nature. Hence, the salesperson's initial picture of the buyer and selling situation will also contain fantasy or projected imagery.

Second, the situations described above may have sounded demeaning to the human decision process. If so, it was only due to oversimplification. This decision process is "as it is"; its complexity is awesome, its capacity for error from inappropriate subconscious imagery is frightening, but its equal capacity for inspired decisions that can transcend the objective data is one of life's highest expressions. This is what we call *wisdom* in its truest sense of the word.

How Does All This Relate to Buying Business Products?

It would be presumptuous to state that this framework is the fundamental explanation of the buying decision process. But I do believe it provides a fresh, sound, and useful way to view the process.

The *rational analysis* of the conscious mind, the *vastness of the experiences* now stored in the personal unconscious, and the *powerful energies* of the archetypical themes of the collective unconscious all go into forming what might be called a *valuing image* in the customer's mind. This valuing image is formed immediately upon initial contact with a company, whether in seeing an ad, reading a brochure, or receiving a personal sales call. It can be net positive or negative. Initially, it has little reality content (the customer probably has not even seen the product), because much personal projected or fantasized content is based upon the unconscious functioning of the psyche just described. As more of the reality unfolds—the customer sees and tries the product, has many more calls from the salesperson, maybe visits the plant— the valuing image likely changes somewhat, reflecting less fantasy and more reality.

Let us now look at the contents of these two modes (fantasy and reality) that make up the valuing image. The first, the *projected or fantasized*, is what we have just discussed, the product of the personal and collective unconscious, and is characterized by hopes, fears, and expectations. It is "dreaming the impossible dream" and can manifest very powerful psychological energy. In male/female relationships it manifests itself by "love at first sight." In buying a car it is the feeling that "when I saw it I knew that it was the car for me." In technical selling it may be the buyer's "knowing" this salesperson or product is going to "give me what I need for me to be seen as *somebody* in this company." Initially the salesperson or product is only a fuse for the fantasy, and hence the term "projection." *The buyer "projects" onto the person or object a personal, inwardly generated imagery that may extend the salesperson's or the product's characteristics far beyond the reality.* This exaggeration will be particularly pronounced if it comes from those powerful themes in the collective unconscious. However, no salesperson can, in the long term, be the hero, father, mother, or god that the ever-questing archetypes demand.

The decline from projection to reality is depressing at best and devastating at worst. Marriage after the honeymoon often requires a different view. The $45,000 car after 5,000 miles drives almost like any other car. The new computer system really hasn't changed the job very much.

This brings us to the other mode, the *real or authentic*, which is the base upon which any continuing relationship must rest.

I will avoid a philosophical discussion on what is reality, if it exists, and suggest that in the kingdom of the mundane reality includes at least the following factors.

- The enhancing factors to the buyer's valuing image:
  - The product itself (which must be of integrity and appropriate to the need as described in Chapter 7).

- Other elements of the marketing mix such as advertising, literature, and promotion (which must be done "right" as described in Chapters 9 through 14).
- The actions of the salesperson (Chapter 8).
- The nature of the salesperson and consequent relationship with the buyer (Chapter 8).
- The depressing factors to the buyer's valuing image:
  - The natural decay of any feeling after the first onslaught, which will continue to erode if there is no re-stimulation.
  - Effects of competitive actions.
  - Distractions.

Let me state my belief that the process of buying/selling is unfathomable, reaching to the roots of our basic nature; and this model is embarrassingly oversimplified. Every situation varies dramatically. However, I do believe this is a useful conceptualization that can be a backdrop as we utilize our combined cognitive and intuitive skills to guide us in the specific situation.

For the visually minded I will attempt to diagram this process. The model is one of a successful, typical, technical sell.

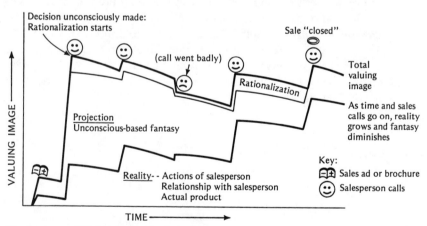

Evolution of Valuing Image Graph

The diagram shows that the decision was made in the first call. However, because the culture of technical buying demands "analysis" and justification, it could not be acknowledged and may not have been conscious. Furthermore, the product may have required testing or even more design; hence, any verbalized or even acknowledged decision would have sounded crazy.

Beneath this conscious rationalization process we see the unconscious-based "projected" energy giving way to the "reality" of the relationship, actions, and product. We see the formal closing or consciously acknowledged decision by the buyer coming when the combination of increased reality and still sufficient fantasy adds up to a high valuing image and the rationalization has reached a self-satisfying state.

By way of contrast, in the typical consumer sale the projection could be at its peak at the start as a result of advertising, and the decision made and acknowledged at that first peak. This is because the cultural need for justification does not necessarily extend to consumer products.

The remaining chapters describe the process of finding out what is needed to design and implement a marketing plan that maximizes both the "reality" portion of the customer's valuing image and, to the extent possible, the projected or fantasy portion.

Your Plan

1. Think of a recent buying decision you made where the alternatives were close and you felt the need to justify the decision. Being perfectly honest with yourself (you don't have to admit this to anyone except yourself), note the emotions that affected the decision. In the final analysis why did you *really* choose as you did?
2. Referring to the preceding diagram, draw a similar one for the decision you just described.

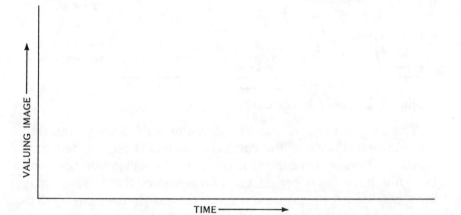

PART
TWO

Designing and Implementing the Marketing Plan

4

The Heart of the Matter—How to Really Know Your Market

T his chapter discusses the most important phase in the marketing cycle, really getting to know your customers (and, collectively, the market).

- Why it is usually not done well.
- What knowledge is needed for an ever-evolving marketing plan.
- Where to find the information.
- The psychology of customers telling you their business.
- Who should do it.

Perspective

The last chapter introduced the idea that technical products are purchased based upon the valuing image the customer creates and that much of this comes from the unconscious and is not "rational." What is triggered in the unconscious is due to stimuli or "igniters" represented by the product, the salesperson, and literature or other communications. Since we do not really know the particular content of any given customer's unconscious (we know very little of our own), we can operate only from some assumptions and clues.

Two assumptions can be made:

- The product must be absolutely appropriate to its actual use.
- It must be sold with the most appropriate marketing plan.

To know what is "most appropriate" in a market we must immerse ourselves in the culture of that market. We must know the five major companies that are the trendsetters and the eight industry gurus who reflect the collective thinking of that market segment. We must understand the way things are marketed, the distribution, the key industry events, and certainly the competition. We must feel the tempo, know the language, and get the market culture into our bloodstream. This is of course necessary when we are deciding whether or not (and if so, how) to introduce a product. Even more importantly, it must continue throughout the life of the product to keep both the product and the marketing strategy attuned to changing needs.

While learning a market (I keep resisting the use of that slightly pompous term "market research") is an absolute necessity, it produces very few strokes of genius or results that merit astonishment. Rather it allows you to do *well* what you are supposed to do. Astonishing happenings may occur as a by-product however. The customer may tell you what is *really* needed—something with many times the potential of what you are asking about. Or you may think of a great idea yourself based upon looking at what is on the customer's table or in the factory (if you are taking the tour you should gently request). Know the technology you are investigating and the questions you want answered *so thoroughly that you can keep part of your attention alert for serendipitous possibilities.*

Learning a market, done properly, is not a matter of boring statistics. Rather it is a vital and exciting interaction with customers and industry resources. With a new product, that inquiring call can be one of the most powerful sales calls made, paving the way for the future time when you are actually trying to make the sale.

While consumer products are often market researched to death (all too frequently still resulting in idiotic products), technology products tend to be insufficiently studied. In the next section we will discuss some reasons for that.

Why Insufficient Market Learning Is All Too Prevalent

According to the gas laws in physics, any amount of gas, no matter how small, will fill its entire container. Likewise a little information will fill our need to know—leaving us quite satisfied and comfortable. This is particularly true in large companies where there is a haphazard flow, often only a trickle, of data coming back from the sales force. However it provides sales and market managers with enough "gas" so they continue to conclude "we know our marketplace."

In new, entrepreneurial situations the inventor's preconception about the market need and exultation at having given birth to a new product may overwhelm any curiosity regarding how the potential customer may see the value of the product.

Shyness plays a key role, and most of us have at least a trace of this affliction. We simply feel we may be "put down" by whomever we are asking, or that they really do not want to spend time answering our questions when we don't even have a finished product.

Fear can hold us back because we do not want to hear bad news. If you have heavily invested yourself emotionally in a product or venture, you will not want to search very hard for someone who might scoff at it.

Busyness is the catch-all excuse. "There is too much for me to do right here trying to get the production design finished, the brochure prepared, and everything else to go chasing around asking a bunch of questions of people who can't even appreciate what I'm trying to do."

Segmentation of the Market

Is there only one market, one product, and one entry level of the product to its market? If so, life is simple; if not, each significant segment must be considered.

- Market application segmentation. Products such as certain test instruments, electronic components, and hydraulic fittings may be sold to several different markets or industries. Each has its own potentials, trends, product and marketing channels, hence each must be examined independently.

- Product segmentation. Are there two or more distinct product variations, such as high-performance, high-cost versions and less critical, price-competitive commodity versions? Each will take a different marketing plan.
- Market entry segmentation. In some cases the same product could enter the market at end user, distributor, and/or OEM (original equipment manufacturer) level. Obviously each entry point has its own needed strategy and hence must be studied as a unique entity.

Information Needed for the Marketing Plan

This of course will vary somewhat from one situation to another, but the following is a good base from which to develop your own list. The sources of the data are listed, but details on how to get the data from the sources are described in following sections. The information should be determined for each segment of the market.

Information	*Source*
Market Size	
Level I • Total market for the field. This would be the family of related products. It is an indication of the size of the total ball field you are playing in and how much room you have to diversify and grow	• Industry journals • Trade associations • Annual reports of companies in the field • Studies by consultants or market research firms • Government reports
Level II • Total for specific product or market under consideration	• Same as above

From these data, coupled with optimizing a "what if" exercise in the marketing plan, the following two additional sets of data will be developed:

Level III • Reachable portion of market for specific product, considering	• The geographical territory, market segment, product segment, entry level, account selection

Information	Source

Market Size (cont.)

specific strategy and resources available	and response to the chosen strategy
Level IV • Realistic growth curve and share of the above	• Add times for product development, sales contacts, customer's decision, and delivery

While Levels III and IV will not be determined until the market plan is developed, it is well to keep these projections in mind while doing the research. You will be more sensitive to making value judgments on ''can I really get half of this company's business?'' and ''how long will it take?''

Industry Trends or Driving Forces

• What is happening to the product or field my product is intended for?	• Users or potential users
	• Industry journals
	• Trade associations
• Sales volume trends	• Published studies by market research firms
• Technological trends	
• Marketing strategy trends	• Industry gurus
• Emerging and dying applications or segments	

Top Customers or Potential Customers

• By name, address, and key people, arrayed in diminishing order of importance	• Industry association membership lists
	• Thomas Register
	• Supplier directories

Competition

• Sales volumes	• Your purchase of their actual product
• Product strengths and weaknesses	
• Company strengths and weaknesses	• Their annual reports and literature
• Marketing strategies	• Market research firms' reports
• Pricing and cost structure	• Trade shows
• How viewed by customers	• Ex-employees
• Proprietary protection	• Users
	• Patent Office search

Information	Source
Product Requirements	
• Details of function it should perform	• Users or potential users
• Environment (heat, humidity, vibration)	• Competition
• Interfacing with adjacent products	
• Human interfacing	
• Size	
• Weight	
• Color	
• Life expectancy	
• Opportunities of extending its function for added value	
• Specifications and approvals (UL, FAA, etc.)	
• Product standardization (vs. customization) possible	
Selling Issues	
• Customers' view of appropriate price	• Users or potential users
• Perceived required "logical" benefits	• Competition
• What benefits make the customer glow, tingle, or be tweaked?	
• Who makes decisions?	
• What is the likelihood *this* particular customer will buy *this* product when it becomes available?	
• If so, how *long* will it take and how *many* sales calls will be required?	
• Product availability expected (from factory, on order, from stock or local distribution)	

Information	*Source*

Selling Issues (cont.)

- Is the product going on an *existing* or proposed program?
- Anticipated usage-timing
- Status of competition at the account
- Service or product support expected
- What trade magazines does customer read and shows do they attend?
- What competitive advertising are they aware of?

- Assessments from your "gut feeling" as you carry on discussions with potential customers. Questions such as "If this performs as we anticipate, what are the chances your company might use it?" can help

Internal Resources

- Technology available to develop, refine or customize the product
- Production capability
- Sales and service people available and territories coverable
- Money available for development, promotion, additional resources, working capital
- Enthusiasm and attitudes
- Difficulties (time, money, lack of talent) to overcome

- The key people inside your own company

How to Get the Information

From Users and Potential Users

Users are your key resource and most of the learning efforts should be spent here. Get on a plane or pick up the phone—*now*. Anyone who thinks that data for a marketing plan can be prepared sitting at a desk reading publications should be banished to the accounting department immediately and forever. The following suggestions should be helpful in pursuing this frightening venture—of going out and actually asking people to help you by telling you how they feel and think.

- People like to be asked. It is not a bother but instead is an ego-booster. You will be amazed at what they will tell you.
- In the culture of U.S. industry, contacts and introductions are *not* necessary. They may be helpful, but don't spend time trying to arrange them. Call directly! And the person should be one step *higher* than you think you need. This way you may get that person's view *plus* an attention-getting reference to the individual you really want to talk to.
- People will talk as much if not more on the phone as they will face to face. The comfortable illusions of control and anonymity tend to free up a telephone communication.
- Open the conversation with directness, candor, and self disclosure.
- Really *ask* questions and *be receptive to* answers. Do not defend the product idea in response to negative comments and do not sell. These attitudes will tend to close down your contact's candor.
- No "canned" speeches: "Hello—I'm taking a survey and would you answer ten questions?" Rather say, "I'm Mabel Gargoyle with Gastric Pneumatic Control Corp." (If they don't know the company, tell where you are located and what the company does.) "We have a new product under development and before we spend any more R&D dollars on it we need some opinions on whether we are going in the right direction." And so on.
- Avoid triggering "proprietary paranoia." State that the information you are giving is not proprietary and that you do not want to touch upon their proprietary areas. Ask potentially sensitive questions in a general way. For example, ask "On an industry-wide basis, who would you think are the major users?" Do *not* ask, "Who are your major customers?" Incidentally, the answers will likely be the same.
- Have your questions well thought out in advance, or perhaps even written, but do not ask them mechanically. Know what you need to find out so well that you intuitively can weave the conversation to cover everything. Note taking during a visit is usually all right and in fact can make your contact feel you value the answers. In your note pad you can have a checklist to glance at as you near the end of the conversation.

- Listen *acutely* for the aside comment, the under-the-breath mutter, the missing answer, the personal problem grumble. These may be clues to a serendipitous opportunity. An answer like "Your new product sounds good, but that's not my problem at the moment" is an unintended invitation to ask what the main problem is. Do ask! *That problem may offer an opportunity twice as big as the one you called about.*
- To determine what benefits make a person "glow, tingle, or be tweaked"—i.e., what gets into the region of igniting deep unconscious themes—watch the body language. Look for a twinkle in the eyes, a self-reflective smile, a glow in the face, a change in body position, particularly one more upright or forward. Likewise, watch for negative expressions.
- If the market or job is unfamiliar, start with a few calls on unimportant potentials to get "in the groove." Then go down the list, starting with the most important (to get maximum data for time spent).
- The person or persons you should talk with at the user company will depend upon the product. Some products could have a widespread enough effect so it would be well to talk with engineering, marketing, production, and purchasing. Generally engineering is key, because they will have to specify the switch to your product. However, if your product alters your customer's product function or appearance, marketing should be visited. If it alters manufacturing methods, production should be consulted. If there would be competition at the buying level, then the views of purchasing should be sought.
- How do you "get through" if you do not know the name? The barriers (if any) will be the switchboard operator, secretaries to lower level managers, and purchasing people, not the people you really want to talk with. Assuming your goal is to talk with the key engineer on "burpleoids," you should ask the switchboard operator for the secretary to the director of engineering. With the response "Mr. Boilfish's office" you simply ask if he is in. (You now have his name.) If he is available, then unravel your story. If not, call back or tell the secretary what you are calling for and ask what person in the department is responsible for "burpleoids." In general, secretaries at the higher management level are quite helpful, as their jobs demand a broader view and a more encompassing function.

- If the switchboard operator, because of "policy," refers you to the purchasing staff when there is no reason for you to talk with them, simply tell them the purpose of the call, ask them some questions in their area (i.e., buying criteria, vendor qualifications, attitudes to sole sources, etc.), then start upgrading the technical content of the questions beyond their knowledge. They will feel flattered you thought they could answer and will usually refer you to the engineer at that point. If instead, they ask you to send a letter with your questions (the ultimate waste), thank them and go to plan two, calling the key *marketing* person. The receptionist will not divert a marketing call to purchasing; the gregarious marketing person will gladly talk to you and then refer you to the engineer.
- A good topic sequence is:

  Your introduction. Tell them what you are trying to do. This "gives" them something.

  Ask about functional requirements. This is safer ground than quantities and prices.

  Quantity and price issues.

  Finally, "What is your purchasing or approval procedure for a product like this?"

- Always ask, "Who else should I talk with?"

From and About Competitors

- First, simply buy their product and dissect it thoroughly.
- The best time and place to talk with competitors is at trade shows. Here you can usually help yourself to literature, see the new products, hear their pitches, maybe get samples, and chat with them during their more loose-lipped periods.
- Friendly customers and distributors are ready sources of literature and product data.
- If all else fails, simply call the competition and ask that information be sent—it usually will be.
- Stock registration information is public data and more detailed than annual reports. Your stock broker can readily obtain it.

From Industry Sources

- Trade publication editors are a fount of information, and very cooperative because they hope to get your future advertising plus a technical article.
- Trade association directors, committee chairpeople, and conference paper presenters are often good starting points for overviews. They tend to know what is going on in the field, who other key contacts might be, and by being in the public eye themselves have shown they either are compulsive talkers, need recognition, or are bloated with data.
- Market research firms publish studies of almost every imaginable field, charge $1,000 to $20,000 for them, and may have a free promotional summary which will provide some of the key information. The trade journal editors are likely to know who has done such studies for a given field.

From Inside Your Company

- Even for marketing data, ask around your own company. You might be surprised how many experts from ''earlier lives'' know a lot about the particular field you are researching.
- Contact both the key person involved and the boss. Approach everyone with the attitude of seeking a partnership in this endeavor vs. ''I'm asking you questions about *my* program.''

Typical Situations

Product Is New or Improved and Market Is Identified But Sales Are Not Yet Being Made

If we take the typical situation of a new company with a product idea or invention, or an existing company wanting to evaluate the feasibility of getting into a new market, the following steps will yield the most data, the most quickly and for the least cost.

- Join the trade organization. Call or visit the director. Ask for all the studies they have done, and others they know about, as well as the key, knowledgeable people in the field, major competitors, and customers (often the membership lists give much of this).

- Obtain the last three years of conference proceedings and scan for articles on market trends, technology trends, recurring authors, or authors that actually have something to say.
- Subscribe to trade journals and obtain, or at least look through, issues from the past three years for market data, technology articles, and names of key people and customers.
- Call or visit the editors of trade journals to obtain market data.
- Prepare a list of the additional information you need.
- Make up a ranked list of important customers. Visit the top ten and telephone an additional 20 or 30.
- Assemble the data on competition.

Product Is New But Market Applications Are Not Known

An example of this situation could be a new plastic resin with properties different from existing products. The question is whether it has enough potential to merit further development.

One way to approach this is to hold a brainstorming session with some of the more creative people from your company and think up all the applications for which the product's unique properties would be useful. Then array these in order of potential based upon the group's conventional wisdom. Pick the top few, research them as previously described, and see if they add up to the threshold that would justify going ahead. If so, utilize a marketing plan (to be detailed in later chapters) that would initially "rifle shoot" the identified markets and "shotgun" for user-generated ideas in additional markets.

Product Still Cannot Be Talked About—Yet You Must Decide Whether to Spend More R&D Money

The first thing to do would be to file a patent application so you can talk about it. If for some reason this is not possible, explain to potential users that you are in the very awkward position of having to research market potential for a product you cannot talk about. (Since they have similar situations, they usually understand.) Then tell them you have to confine the conversation to

nonconfidential areas, which means *functional* needs and performances vs. *how* it works. For example, you can ask if 150°C performance is of interest to them, or if a tensile strength greater than 20,000 psi is needed, without telling them how you are achieving it.

Product Is Already Being Marketed and You Want to Keep Ahead

This is one place a questionnaire to your sales force may be useful and appropriate. It should not take the place of your *very frequent* direct conversations with key customers and salespeople. At the customer level, seek comments from *actual users*. This could mean the assembly-line worker or field installation person. Do not rely on the engineer or purchasing agent.

Also watch the competition *very* closely.

Product Is So Revolutionary That Customers' Products or Work Habits Must Be Radically Changed to Utilize It

A classic example is the Xerox machine, where it has been said an initial survey indicated a market for fewer than 100 machines. Other examples might be the personal computer, the airplane, or solar power. Incidentally, such situations are quite rare as most even seemingly radical products replace something being done functionally by a different method.

The approach here is to pray for the intuitive wisdom of the inventor and more so for the investor.

Who Should Gather the Data?

• Someone thoroughly knowledgeable in the subject being researched. More than just learning *about* the product or technology, the data gatherer should have spent more time in *active, physical* development or testing of it. The "aliveness" this gives to the interviewer's knowledge is invaluable in recognizing subtleties in responses and pursuing avenues of inquiry not in the initial "script." This means the person should not be a contract consultant provided with a questionnaire, a summer student you do not know what to do with, or a trainee sent out to get a feel for the market.

• Probably not the inventor alone. The inventor *should* go on a number of calls to hear the reactions directly, but the wise inventor will take a more objective, but knowledgeable, person along so that balanced questions will be asked and interpretations of responses can be compared.

• Someone who has had selling experience. A sales background may help to identify biases that come out of the "asking questions" situation versus an actual sales encounter. The two most common biases are exhibited by (1) the person who cannot envision the eventual product from the description, the sketches, or prototype and hence tends to be negative; or (2) the overly exuberant type who loves being asked for an opinion, and may have an exaggerated image of the end product. However, if later faced with the frightening, committing decision to buy or not to buy, this latter type can through personal insecurities or through organizational resistance become a difficult buyer. Selling experience is no guarantee for perceiving such biases, but it may develop a certain sensitivity to them. Furthermore, I would like to think an experienced salesperson's "gut feeling" about the probability of the customer ultimately buying and length of time required to do so would be better than that of someone without the experience.

• Someone who is personable and an extremely sensitive listener. Here we may take a little excursion into some psychology to identify who should *not* be doing the customer interviews. The terms "extrovert" and "introvert" are widely used and are often misused when compared to Jung's original definitions. In Jung's notion, extroverts look outward for their life-sustaining data—listening, observing, and forming their values and order from the world about. By contrast, introverts depend more upon inner imagery. In fact, all people have some of each but vary in the proportions. Popular usage of the terms has loud-mouths identified as extroverts and quiet people as introverts—a quite insufficient and usually inaccurate simplification.

A boring, nonstop talker is likely an introvert who unfortunately lacks sufficient shyness to keep this loutish behavior in check. Inappropriate and flat-out tiring chatter is the product of internal imagery—extremely exciting to the talker but not in tune with anyone else.

An interesting loudmouth, or on a lesser scale a gregarious person, may be extroverted, with this extroversion providing sufficient audience feedback to keep the oration tolerable. This kind of behavior is usually a compensation for some lack of confidence, weak ego, or lack of self-identity. Somehow the person feels that flap and flailing will win acceptability. In this process of compensating, much of the information and the pleasure that an extroverted sensitivity is capable of garnering from the outside world is lost.

The shy introvert cannot successfully do market research because even with an A in "overcoming shyness training" such a person would still not really care what the customer thought—the introvert's own image is all that matters. Introverts also tend to create their own images of outside situations. For example, I recall a very talented introverted scientist telling me how the customer, whom he had never met, would logically accept a delay in a new program because he had read they had their own delay in a product introduction. Of course this little fantasy of logic had no relation to the reality of the situation and proved to be quite wrong.

Such extreme types obviously are not suited to do well in the data gathering interview. The ideal person is extroverted and confident enough to listen carefully and question appropriately. These people look, listen, intuit, and tend to take aboard the attitudes surrounding them. How do you know this personality? While psychological tests, in particular the Meyers Briggs, are thought to be valid in detecting introversion versus extroversion, my view is that one rely on judgment tempered with caution.

Organizational Considerations

In a start-up company based on a single new product, the head of marketing should gather data, and should be accompanied on at least eight to ten key calls by the inventor or technical head. Furthermore the key manufacturing person should have exposure to potential customers.

In a larger company someone who reports to the product or market manager would be a logical choice, and again would involve both technical and manufacturing people in a number of the key visits.

Your Plan

1. What, if any, inhibitions do you feel about visiting (or telephoning) potential customers to ask about their needs in relation to your potential products? Try also to identify the cause of the inhibitions.
2. What market segment(s) do you intend to address?
3. Prepare your list of topics appropriate to what you need to know further about this product. Think through and note how you might ask the questions.

5

Making Sense
out of This Information

T his chapter tells you how to know if you have learned enough to get the product started and how to distill what you have learned in the areas of:

- Market potential
- Product requirements
- Required marketing strategy
- Ethical issues

Some analysis is done instinctively in the gathering of data, while most is done while developing the strategy and marketing plan. Therefore, I will cover only a few selected topics on the subject of analysis in this short chapter. In one sense this chapter is a checkpoint to see if you have gathered enough data. It is also a point in the marketing cycle where you ask, "Should I continue to pursue this product idea?"

Market Potential

If in your research of industry literature you have found two significantly different values for the same statistic, call the authors and try to learn how they arrived at their figures. Use what seems most solidly supported.

Much more important is to try to arrive at your own figures by extrapolating from specific customer data you have gathered. For example, the five major potential users for a certain size disc drive have told you their requirements, and they represent 30% of the market. See how this potential divided by .30 compares to the "industry" figures from the trade journals or market research firms' multiclient studies. If it is much lower, check with the authors of the studies. If they do not have a good explanation, you had better use the more conservative number. For each of the customers contacted, estimate: What is the probability of a sale? What is the overall average? How long will it take to make a typical sale from time of initial contact? How many personal sales calls will be needed during this time?

Calculating Levels III and IV

From the data gathered, you proceed from Level II (total market for the specific product, as discussed in Chapter 4) to Level III (reachable level) by multiplying Level II by all the factors that limit the product's market penetration. For example: Level II for an electrical connector is $10 million. List the factors and estimate, based upon data gathered, the percent of the total resulting from each of these limiting factors.

Factor	Value
Geographical (U.S. only)	.40 (only 40% in U.S.)
Market application segment (computer only)	.70 (of all applications, computers are 70%)
Product segment (high performance only)	.60
Market entry segment (direct sales to OEMs only)	.50 (half go through distributors)
Customer responsiveness (consider competition, need, timing, general attitude)	.30 (30% of the customers contacted indicated they might buy)

Level III = $10 mil × .40 × .70 × .60 × .50 × .30 = $252,000.

Now you can move on to Level IV (realistic growth curve) and consider time to train and place the salespeople, the number of calls they can make once in place, and buying cycle times (usually longer for new product). Place the results of this on a time scale to obtain a growth curve.

Product Requirements

Sort and evaluate the data regarding product requirements from the following viewpoints.

- Customer reactions
- Competitive data
- Your technical innovations
- Your firm's manufacturing capability

Obviously, data from the larger potential customers or particularly knowledgeable sources should be given more weight. As a test of the adequacy of your data, *write a draft of the sales brochure and product specification,* including a sketch of the product showing its functional details. For example, if it is an instrument, show controls and readouts, their scales and locations. The specification should include a list of all the performance characteristics that are important. As a guide to the topics, look at competitive literature and review the features the customer seems to emphasize.

If you cannot fill in all the answers on the above draft, you most likely will want to call back some of the potential customers you contacted earlier and/or some new ones. In some cases, certain details may be unanswerable—and you will have to rely on your judgment.

Required Marketing Strategy

First compile a list of strengths and weaknesses of the major competitors, their products, strategies, and reputations—along with the same for your own firm. Note the areas where they are weak and you are strong. The following may be used as a guide in compiling your list of comparative issues.

	Competition			Your Company (Including possible resources additions)
	Co. A	Co. B	Co. C	
The People				
Overall caliber				
Training				
Ethics				
Response to customers				
The Company				
Financial strength				
Manufacturing capability				
Product development capability				
Responsiveness to market changes				
Products				
Technical leadership				
Quality				
Reliability				
Cost "floor"				
Proprietary protection				
Marketing				
Performance of sales-people				
Prices				
Distribution				
Strong and weak market segments				
Service				
How seen by customer				

From this pick a *path of vulnerability* where the competition is weak but you have or can obtain strengths. Then from all the data available, list the various alternative forms of "connection" or contact with the customer that can bring about the sale. Completing the following statement may be helpful.

This product can be sold by (details of training and personal characteristics) calling on (customer type, the specific roles of the people involved in the decision), by saying (the key thrust of the sales story) aided by the following communication supplements (literature, advertising, trade shows, direct mail, etc.) and supplied by (distributor, factory direct) at the price of ($).

Often there is only one answer at this point. In fact, to an experienced marketing person in an industrial or technology area, the single best strategy usually becomes readily apparent. However, if this is not the case, write the two or three that seem viable alternatives. Examples of a strategy summary statement might be:

- These semiconductor testing systems must be sold by sales engineers with thorough electrical engineering backgrounds plus at least six months factory training; to the major semiconductor companies; requiring the approval of the heads of manufacturing, quality control, and purchasing. The unique "edge" is the system's ability to test 30% faster, and the modular design allows our firm to "customize" the installation in one half the time of the specially designed competitive units. Sales will be aided by very detailed instruction and service data. The system will be shown at the SEMICON show. Distribution will be factory direct only. Prices can be 10% above competition.
- This new industrial tape line with its low creep at high temperatures will be sold through trade advertising to the end user, coupled with an intensive "selling" of the leading industrial distributors by our factory people. Introduction incentives will be given to distributors to insure display space and selling effort by the distributor salespeople. Prices should be the same as the competition.

You now have a very rough statement of strategy which will be filled out and fine tuned when we discuss "strategy" in the following chapter.

Ethical Issues

List all the positive and negative economic, environmental, sociological, and personal impacts the existence of the product will make upon customers, your firm, your suppliers, the community, and yourself. Answer these questions:

- Should this product exist?
- Should my company be involved with this product?
- Should I be involved with it, considering my personal values?

Finally, check with the other members of your team to be sure you are in general agreement. Disagreements on issues at this level, which are often not discussed, can surface in other guises and be very troublesome.

Wisdom and Judgment (or, Where Analysis Stops)

I recently reviewed the resumés of the graduating class from a highly regarded business school, and found nearly half the class had noted in their qualifications "proven analytical skills." I thought, "how admirable, yet how naive and even downright foolish." It was as though they thought this is where the world stops—rather than just starts.

The most profound analyses have never resulted in anything more than doing well what you should have done all along. By its very nature, analysis is incapable of creation, breakthrough, or profound insight. At most, it can identify the windows of opportunity for invention, wisdom, or insight. These functions in turn draw heavily from the unconscious.

Therefore, once analysis is done (and, one hopes, done well), it is time to sit back, look at the analytical results, then listen to your intuition. Call upon that most noble of human traits, wisdom, and the most demanding, judgment, by asking "what really makes sense?"

What can we say about the nature of wisdom and judgment? In James Hillman's writing on "senex consciousness,"[1] or the attitudes often associated with the views from old age (senility), he contrasts such attitudes with puer (or youthful) consciousness and its adventuresomeness. (Incidentally, these polarities are not necessarily related to chronological age.) Both these attitudes have a positive and negative component. My extrapolation and simplification of Hillman's notion are shown here in diagram form. The encircled area is the region where successful marketing judgments are made. Too high on the vertical axis and to the left

[1]James Hillman, "Senex and Puer: An Aspect of the Historical and Psychological Present," *Eranos Jahrbuch XXXVI*, Zurich (Rhein), 1968.

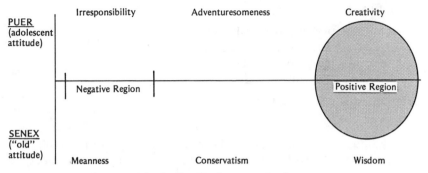

| | Irresponsibility | Adventuresomeness | Creativity |

PUER
(adolescent
attitude)

Negative Region   Positive Region

SENEX
("old"
attitude)

Meanness   Conservatism   Wisdom

Marketing Judgment Scale

side of the diagram is too risky, and too far below and left is too limiting or conservative.

How do we measure this? I know of no "analytical" way. It is a real test of wisdom and good judgment to know if someone's psyche falls within the positive region and even a greater test to know if your own does.

The wisest of us can get in the grip of our hero archetype in the same fashion described in Chapter 3 in reference to the customer. This can position us up and to the left in the diagram, where our judgments may be of sufficient risk at least to deserve review by someone who will "level" with us. If we are lucky, we all have that type of friend.

These notions on the application of wisdom and judgment apply throughout the entire process of marketing (as well as to the rest of life).

Your Plan

1. Can you answer?	Published reports	Extrapolation of customer data
a. Size of Level I market (field of products)	_____	_____
b. Size of Level II market (specific products)	_____	_____

2. Trends.

3. Profile of sale:

    a. average probability of sale per
       potential customer _____

    b. no calls required _____

    c. buying cycle time _____

4. Write the "sales story" for the brochure.

5. Calculate Level III.

From the data gathered, multiply Level II results by all the factors that limit the product's market penetration. List the factors and estimate the percent of the total resulting from each.

Factor   Value (% of Level II)

—Geographical

—Market Application Segment

—Product segment

—Customer responsiveness (consider competition, need, timing, general attitude)

Level III = Level II × Value of each factor
                   above

6. Estimate Level IV

Consider time to train and place the sales people, the number of calls they can make, and buying cycle times. Use the results to prepare a time scale and growth curve.

7. Product specifications:

    a. draw sketch (if appropriate)
    b. list product specifications
    c. complete the draft of the sales brochure

8. Fill out a chart on competition like the one presented in this chapter.

9. Write the first draft of a strategy statement (use format examples from this chapter).

10. Ethical issues:

    a. should this product exist? _____
    b. should my company be involved with this? _____
    c. should *I* be involved with this? _____

11. A calibration of your judgment.

    Mark where you think you are on the following scale.

	Irresponsibility	Adventuresomeness	Creativity
PUER (adolescent attitude)			
	Negative Region		Positive Region
SENEX ("old" attitude)	Meanness	Conservatism	Wisdom

6

Honing Your Goal and Developing Your Strategy

T his is the first of eight chapters discussing the design of the marketing plan. Whether it is being done for the first time with a new product, or as part of the continual review that is vital to the success of an ongoing product, the process is the same. Based on your learning the market and analyzing your findings (Chapters 4 and 5), you must reassure yourself the goal is do-able, the strategy is correct in terms of customer expectations, trends, and competition (this chapter), the product is appropriate (Chapter 7), and the strategy (the marketing mix) is played in the right proportions (Chapters 8 through 14).

The marketing plan summary sheet, which actually is an abbreviated projected profit and loss budget, is a good way to visualize where this is all leading. It is discussed in detail in Chapter 16. After this summary sheet we will go immediately into the review of your earlier established goal and then discuss strategies.

Goals

In Chapter 2 you had your dream and from it forged a goal. Now that you have learned your market and analyzed the relevant in-

The Marketing Plan Summary Sheet

Goal: _____

Strategy: _____

The product description: _____

	$000/year		
	1	2	3
Market potential			
The field (Level I)			
Specific product (II)			
Available (III)			
Sales forecast (IV) Cost of goods sold			
Gross margin			
Expenses R&D G&A Marketing (include description of each activity) Sales Distribution Service Literature Advertising Publicity Trade shows Conventions Seminars			
Total marketing expense			
Total expenses			
Profit before taxes			

formation, you should reexamine and, if necessary, refine the goal. Check the definition of the product, market area, and the five-year targets.

Regarding the qualitative portion, you should have a solid enough value system so this does not change. However, now is a good time to review it again.

Strategies

The strategy is the *way* to get to the goal. Whereas goals are established with an arbitrary passion, then fine tuned with logic, strategies are created through a logical process. While creativity and insight should be brought to bear as much as possible, a strategy can be developed through a sequential process to be described shortly.

First, however, I must vent a few words of cynicism on the current popular usage of the words "strategy" and "strategic"— terms touted by consultants and writers and hungrily gobbled up by frustrated management. To understand their popularity we first must look at the paradoxical world of management. On one hand it is laden with demonstrable power—subordinates quake at pronouncements and grovel for even meager recognition. Vacuous management statements are quoted in business presses, and being "an executive" is the current prestige occupation. On the other hand, management really is a journey in uncertainty, fear, and impotency—one's job is at the mercy of higher management or the board of directors; market shifts or unforeseen competition may turn next fiscal year into a disaster; the union may shut down the plant; subordinates never really do what is desired; there may be a raid on the company's stock. Then there is the ever-irritating question—are we really in the right business, and if so is it with the right products, right methods, at the right time? To add to these, managers may have weight problems, underachieving children, or a lackluster love life. To compensate for such failings and to attempt to maintain the fantasy of power come the physical trappings—the big office, big car, first class travel perks, sycophants, and even the ultimate toy and symbol of virility—the private jet. These may help momentarily on the obesity, childrearing, and erotica fronts, but not on the matter of deciding what to do next. This is where strategy comes in. Ah, strategy—with its implications of clarity and power. Rooted solidly in military terminology, strategy suggests clear, crafty, and precise plans resulting in devastating defeat of the opposition and brilliant achievement of objectives. No wonder consultants offer strategic planning services, business writers title their rehashes "Strategic Implications of ———" and even businesses' own plans are more often than not titled "Strategic Growth Plan."

So much for this tirade against the strategic hype. Let us now see how to plan the practical strategy—again defined as simply an intelligent, well-thought-out path to your goal.

In your analysis of the data (Chapter 5) you prepared a general strategy statement based upon market opportunity, your strengths, and competitive weaknesses. Here we are simply going to critique and refine it by examining the following elements.

Account Selection

First, be sure you are very clear who the customer is. Start by identifying the actual end *user.* Then be sure to identify with equal clarity the customer or customers you have to sell to get your product to the user, since the two may be different. For example, as a printed circuit board manufacturer, your user is the operator of the computer. However, your customer is the manufacturer of the "box," such as a printer, that this board is used in. This manufacturer may sell the "box" to the systems company who in turn sells to the user. In this case the strategy certainly should be to direct your effort to the "box" manufacturer. However, if you are new, and particularly if there is something functionally advantageous about your product, the strategy might well include some effort toward assuring the systems company that the final product is reliable. Also they might even exercise some "pull" on the box manufacturer to use your boards. However, it would be of no value to advertise or promote your product to the computer user.

On the other hand, if you are the manufacturer of a printer or some unit the user *can* identify, then the strategy might well include some advertising to that end user even though your customer is the systems firm.

Once this is clear, then decide how to introduce the product:

- Selectively or generally
- Regionally, nationally, or internationally

The considerations are:

- *Your resources.* Sales coverage, service, and manufacturing capability all must be thoroughly carried out. All have big appetites for working capital.

- *Technical state of product.* It is often a good idea to place a new product in a few test sites to be sure there are no bugs.
- *Competition.* In opposition to above, potential competition suggests moving as widely and as quickly as possible, since once in a test site you have ''tipped your hand.'' Also regarding the influence of competition, you may want to introduce the product first where competition is weakest to allow a rapid initial market penetration.
- *Timing.* These considerations suggest a rapidly accelerating but *do-able* timetable of scale up.

Market Entry Level

Your product will be sold to one or more of the following:

- The OEM (original equipment manufacturer)
- The end user (or end customer)
- Distributors or dealers
- The after market

In many cases, the nature of the product automatically determines entry level. Printed circuit boards, being components of computers, must be sold to OEMs. With other products this is not the case. For example, a medical disposables manufacturer has the choice of selling to hospitals directly or to other manufacturers who in turn sell to hospitals.

Selling to OEMs builds unit volume the fastest with the lowest sales cost since there are fewer customers. However, prices are the lowest, and the loss of one customer can have substantial impact. In general, selling directly to the end user/customer is far more costly, and takes longer to build volume, than selling to OEMs. However, it provides something of much greater value, including a higher unit price, much less vulnerability to competition, and less impact from the loss of a single customer.

The issue of selling through distributors is heavily influenced by the structure of the particular market and is covered in Chapter 10.

''After market'' usually means repair and replacement, and this is usually dictated by the nature of the product and the prior entry level decision.

Looking for vulnerability in your competitors' entry level strategy may be helpful. For example, if the competition is relying on selling through a distribution level and has little direct end-customer contact, you may be able to unnerve them severely by going direct to the key accounts.

Key Accounts

In most cases it is well to prioritize key or strategic accounts. In so doing, use the following factors:

- Size
- Influencing position (degree to which each is an industry trendsetter)
- Timing of their purchase vs. your readiness
- Similarity of their needs and your product goals
- "Chemistry" of working with them

Pricing

Commercial and Industrial Products. First and last rule: Your costs plus budgeted margin is only the floor beneath which you probably do not want to drop, and *has nothing else to do with your price.* Pricing is a delicate balance of the following factors:

- Actual value to the customers; i.e., time or materials saved.
- Perceived value by the customers. They may compute the saving differently from the way you do, or the product may just not look like it should cost that much.
- Competition. Here your uniqueness and how well that uniqueness can be protected determine what, if any, premium can be charged.
- Industry Practices. In the semiconductor industry, very high initial prices for new devices are accepted. (They may drop rapidly thereafter.) In other fields this would be seen as improper and be bitterly resented by early users.

The answer to pricing lies in that wonderful area of wisdom and judgment.

Products or Contract Work for the Government. In this situation government guidelines dictate the calculations of pricing. The latest editions should be obtained and followed carefully.

Protection

A number of tools are available and should be used singularly or together as appropriate.

- *Patents.* In general, "go for them." They do make life more difficult for competition. Also, if you ever do sell the business or the product line, they are an asset upon which valuation can be rationalized. There are, however, some negatives. Cost can run from $2,000 to $20,000 per patent, plus annual maintenance costs. If you file internationally, do so only in major countries—Japan, the United Kingdom, France, Germany. This is likely enough to screw up the market for anyone else. Second, certain products whose uniqueness depends upon formulation or novel manufacturing processes may be best protected by secrecy. Process patents are hard to enforce.
- *Marketing preeminence.* The position of IBM in the computer world is an obvious example. A "me too" product can be marketed readily through their powerful sales force, and an outsider has a very difficult time. However, even a small company can be the first in a unique or emerging market, and the tying up of key distributors (if appropriate) and stunning performance with key customers can make the world difficult for those who follow.
- *Process secrets.* As mentioned earlier, novel manufacturing or formulations that are difficult to analyze (for example, key ingredients are vaporized in subsequent steps) are best protected by secrecy.
- *Timing.* The company which is "firstest with the mostest" may gain a difficult-to-match position. However, other scenarios are also possible. Company A is first, but stumbles; Company B is more agile, capitalizes on A's mistakes, and moves in before A recovers.
- *Specification influence.* Government agencies as well as private companies write specifications to which their purchases must perform. They usually want the state-of-the-art product, so it is often possible to convince them to write the new specification to the latest "state of the art," which incidentally only you happen to be able to supply.
- *Pricing.* If a company has low manufacturing costs, tight expense control, and strong marketing, it may be able to price low enough to achieve its own profit goals but make the opportunity for a new competitor difficult. Unless the product is virtually a commodity, this generally is not a desirable strategy—more often it is a good way to lose money.

Correctly Aiming the Strategy

The aim should be toward *satisfying the customers' need*, first, foremost, and always, instead of aping what competition is doing. Now this is a subtle and difficult distinction to make, because competitive activity is a life or death matter to any business and the actions of its competitors can influence the customers' perceived needs. Perhaps the best way to proceed is first to lay out a strategy that considers only ideally meeting the customers' needs and opportunities, and *then* factor in the influence of competition.

The point I am trying to establish here is that a lemming-like chase that takes an entire pack of suppliers away from making the product most suitable to its application must be avoided. An example of this was automobile digital dashboard gadgetry, which started with push buttons instead of knobs, led to digital speedometers and fuel gauges, and culminated in the trip computer. Each manufacturer plunged headlong into out-digitizing competitors until a few of them came to the realization that people like to turn knobs, see analog readouts, and find trip computers worthless. In the short term a competitively reactive strategy may work (and in a few instances may be necessary) but I do not believe it is successful in the long term.

Special Marketing Situations

While the fundamentals of this book can be applied to any marketing situation, selling the business product to the business buyer in the United States is the general theme. To aid in tailoring strategies to some situations other than this one, I am providing a few comments on the uniqueness of those business environments.

Marketing Outside the United States

In general, the same principles, perspective, and frame of reference apply as for the U.S. environment. However, there are likely to be some differences in specifics:

- Data gathering may be more difficult with "cold" calls, particularly by phone. Introductions may be beneficial in some countries.
- Strategy and marketing mix may be skewed slightly from their U.S. counterparts. Sales agents and distributors may have a different importance, and governments may be a bigger factor in some decisions. Advertising and literature must be prepared by bilingual natives so they are in the cultural mode of the country and not just a U.S. translation. For example, in some countries the standard paper size is not our $8\frac{1}{2}"$ × 11". In certain Far East countries, advertising typically stresses company stability and longevity over specific products as compared to U.S. practices.

In the ideal top management organization, each individual country's subsidiary is run by a native who also has some U.S. education and experience. In turn, the U.S. person to whom this person reports should speak the language fluently and be well traveled and well read in the country. While readings regarding the business, economic, and technical matters are vital, the deeper understanding comes from studying the history, culture, politics, art, and great literature. The great or timeless literature of any country provides insight like none other, since it is a metaphor of the psyche that may be easier to interpret than the art or music.

Operationally, local laws and practices must be fully understood and followed to the letter. Local customs also should be carefully understood and practiced in all instances except where they violate ethical principles such as those relating to bribery or discrimination.

Middle management and technical people should be from the local country to the extent possible. However, there should be considerable mutual visiting or limited work assignments between the local people and U.S. counterparts to promote a spirit of "us" rather than "them".

Marketing of Services

This section discusses some specific aspects of marketing strategies where the product is a service function such as management consulting, advertising, accounting, or recruiting.

Gathering Information and Defining Your Product

Here you must blend two key factors—the specific skills you bring to the task and the specific needs of the potential clients. People first getting into consulting or a similar service frequently make the mistake of billing themselves as all things to all people in a flailing attempt to get some bread on the table.

Start by carefully and honestly listing those specific skills and experiences that set you apart from others—where, given the opportunity, you are a shining star and are totally energized when exercising these skills. Then make a second list of things that you can do competently but are not your first choices. Finally, make a third list of skill resources available to you from associates or people you could hire into your group.

The next step is to survey the market. Call potential customers and speak to their highest level person appropriate to your service. Tell them you are planning to offer consulting services in their field and would like to get their advice in most usefully structuring your services. In the course of low-keyed, non-selling conversations, cover such topics as:

- How much they now use such outside services.
- If they don't use them, why not.
- If they do, what is their experience with them—both satisfactions and disappointments.
- What they know about other firms in the field and what their image of them is.
- If they were to have future needs, what specifically might be required.

From these two areas forge your product definition—biased toward exploiting your very specific skills in an area where there appears to be market opportunity.

Selling Your Services

This is a matter of direct personal contact with the top officer of the potential client company. If your service is the recruiting of salespeople, your customer is the vice president of sales. If accounting, it is the vice president of finance; if acquisitions, it should be the president. Such decisions generally are *really* made by line versus staff management. For example, in the case of sales recruiting, the sales vice president in most cases really carries the clout to use your services, despite much talk about Personnel or Human Resources being the department with whom you must work. The ideal selling tactic here is to try to see the sales vice president first, let him or her bring in Human Resources, then work with both. Likewise, if you have an advertising agency the first "cold" call should be to the vice president of marketing, and then the company advertising director.

In the "sales" part of the mix, referrals by noncompeting service firms can be *very* helpful door openers. For example, if you specialize in marketing consulting or computer systems, a referral by a respected CPA firm can be very helpful. Cultivate these potential referrals by "networking" your acquaintances, by attending industry association meetings, and by direct calls on the firms, telling them you want to let them know you and your services in case their clients could use such referrals.

Your greatest sales potential may be additional work with existing clients, and this should be the object of much but careful sales attention. Principles to follow in this regard are:

- Work in a manner as helpful, interactive, and "team-like" as possible so you become seen almost as one of the employees, and hence someone people depend upon and do not want to see leave.
- Meet as many people as possible. Use the topic of your study or whatever to call people and solicit their views of the situation. Also when you see new people at the coffee pot, introduce yourself, find out what they do, and let them know who you are.
- After finishing a project, follow up—even offering a little free additional time to aid in implementation.
- Where you see a definable opportunity for further work, ask the key people if they would like to have you submit a proposal. Then discuss the situation enough so you have a specific idea what they might expect.
- Ask satisfied clients at the end of the project if they could provide you any referrals to other branches of the company or other companies.

A word of caution regarding extending work with existing clients. Be extremely sensitive to the danger of being parasitic—seemingly more interested in the next job than the one you are on, or trying to create a job where there really is not one. The revulsion such behavior causes is very difficult ever to overcome.

Advertising and Promotion

In this entire area it is first necessary to understand the culture of the particular situation to determine what distinguishes schlock from class, since in many cases it is quite arbitrary. Consulting engineers can advertise in a trade journal, but industrial psychologists cannot. Personnel agencies dealing with technical or lower level people can advertise in the newspaper, but "executive search" firms dealing only in very high level jobs would demean themselves by such practices. Also, there is the risk of overexposure in areas that otherwise ring of "class." For example, presenting a paper or being chairperson at the industry meeting can be most prestigious. However, too many such appearances at too many meetings can hint that you are not doing so well.

Within the limits just described, the following is a menu from which you might select appropriate promotional aids.

- *Articles.* A thought-provoking article in the respected journal of the particular field is always good to establish you as "expert." The more frequent "state of the art summary" article may not do any harm, but is not particularly helpful toward catapulting you into a position of instant esteem in the field.
- *Speeches.* Again, a well done presentation of substance, presented to an esteemed trade club, can be very helpful in getting known and even being sought out.
- *Seminars.* Organizing and conducting such an event can be very helpful. Perhaps an ideal format is to get it sponsored by or affiliated with the trade association or a university for prestige reasons, then ask senior people from your potential clients to be presenters.
- *Advertising.* In those situations where a direct ad might seem in questionable taste, an "announcement" ad has come to the fore.

Kirkletard, Moywinkle and Fardbuster
are pleased to announce that
EMILE MARBLEDOME
is now affiliated with the firm as Senior Consultant.

This is a way of implying that great talent has been added to already great talent, as well as simply "getting your name out there." I find it only slightly less contrived and revolting than the realtors and insurance firms that create "Chairman Club Awards." They take a large ad to inform the world that the grinning teeth belong to "Myra Pondolliper, distinguished professional in your area." However, such ads are harmless and if the culture of your profession respects them, why not.

- *Brochures.* In all cases a well done, conservatively stated brochure of your offered services and the backgrounds of the key people is necessary. This can be used as a direct mail piece where appropriate, as well as something to leave with a potential client.

Start High

Your image will be established quickly by the circle you travel in, and it is hard to "trade up." Try to get as first clients those firms who are highly respected. Likewise, be selective in the groups you address and publications for whom you write.

Marketing to Government Agencies

The network of people that must be sold may be far reaching and *all* must be sold in a coordinated way. Specifications may be written at one government location after testing is done at another. Approved vendor lists may be still another department's responsibility. Procurement may be by a subcontractor only after the prime contractor has approved it, and installation may be at a totally different location than either. A slip anywhere and the entire program can come crashing down (or not even get off the ground). For example, installation difficulty at the manufacturing site can be communicated (distorted and magnified) to the vendor approval department and you are out in the cold.

Most government people are very friendly, helpful folks who enjoy having associations with the "private sector" as they quaintly call it. However, many live in mortal fear that some action of theirs will get them criticized by their superiors. So, start at the top. If the bosses are presold, they cannot criticize or even question a decision in your favor by the person responsible. Second, be very sensitive to the risk level of the decision you are asking someone to make. Don't overload them.

Government specifications rule the decisions and you can use this to your advantage by having them upgraded to reflect your product's advantages. This gives the agency the latest and best while barring competitors who make inferior products. To accomplish this upgrade requires relationship in the best sense of the word, namely close interaction on a base of trust, integrity, and mutual understanding as well as frustrating hours on industry/government committees and task forces.

One of the first things to check, to avoid wasting your time and effort, is whether or not the program is funded and if so, at what level—feasibility study, prototype, or production.

Recent rulings regarding pricing, vendor relations, and influence must be thoroughly understood. These can be obtained from government contracting agencies.

Your Plan

1. Restate your goal now that you have some data.
2. Reexamine the strategy and define the following issues.
   a. account selection
   b. entry level
   c. pricing
   d. protection
   —patents
   —marketing strengths
   —process secrets
   —timing
   —specifications
   —others you may see

Products—The Basis of It All

We are now ready to formulate the marketing plan or "marketing mix" as it is often called. This marketing mix is the "fleshing out" or detailing of the *strategy* which might be viewed as the *framework that defines the basic thrust*.

The product is the key ingredient of the marketing plan. While this may seem like a trite, self-evident statement, all too often the marketing plan is looked upon as an independent entity, distinct from the product—which is seen as being in the domain of the engineers. As entrepreneur, product manager, or marketing manager, *your* responsibility is to insure on a continual basis that the product is both profitable and most appropriate to the customers' needs. This is the basis upon which the marketing mix is built.

We often hear of "market pull" or "technology push" products—terms that oversimplify the complex reality. No "technology push" is going to succeed in an unreceptive market; no "market pull" is going to demand a product that is not yet technically conceived. A better description is the concept of a "dance" between the technology and the market. Like partners in a dance, there may be some mismatch until the rhythms of each are mutually learned, but then, if the timing is right, a "magical" event can occur. In this chapter we will discuss the special interaction between technology and marketing that lets this magic happen.

Scientific Research, Technology, and Product Development

First let us clarify the differences between these pursuits.

Scientific research is attempting to extend our understanding of physical existence. The discovery of elements, the understanding of the atomic structure, and the characterizing of electrical properties of materials are a few examples. The process is one of discipline, then intuition, and then return to discipline. First a thorough study of what is known is made, and with this as a backdrop an intuitive leap is made in the form of a hypothesis or a tentative forecast of what might be. Then comes discipline again as appropriate tests are designed and carried out to prove or disprove this hypothesis.

Technology development is the taking of scientific knowledge and applying it to perform a new function—or to improve an existing function. The decrease in size of the semiconductor junction, allowing more and more of them to be put on a chip, is a well known example. The process typically consists of a series of alternating disciplined and intuitive steps as experiments are designed, carried out, reformulated—often with an intuitive leap (or hunch)—then repeated, with each iteration ratcheting the technologist closer to the goal.

Product development involves dipping into this stream of technology development and configuring it into a useful product. Expanding upon the previous example, the development of new generations of computer chips, with their ever astounding capabilities, represents product development resulting from technology development's further reduction of the junction size. Another level of product development is the computer itself or other equipment using this chip.

The product development process may typically consist of:

1. The understanding of market data
2. Survey of the current state of technology
3. The intuitive vision
4. The logical process of laying out the design of this vision
5. Modeling functional elements
6. Detailed calculations
7. "System" design
8. Prototyping, testing, and redesigning
9. Repeats of any or all of the above steps

Where Products Come From

In a new company there are as many sources and reasons for the existence of the product as there are entrepreneurs. Every invention is a marvelous story and is an inherent part of the character of the inventor, usually reflecting some long-standing work or hobby interest. The product is the "precious child" of the inventor, who maintains blind belief in its viability. It is this belief, coupled with inexhaustible energy, that drives the product to its success, or the too frequent expensive failure. Needless to say, this is where market knowledge *early enough* in the development program, can increase the probability of success and reduce losses.

In an ongoing company the best source of opportunities is your *existing* customers. This rich source is tapped into by developing strong, lasting relationships with them and listening, listening, and listening more to their needs. In their plants, be constantly looking for opportunities. If they speak about their problems, ask for more information—it may be a new product opportunity.

If there is evidence of an opportunity, bring in your creative technical person so his or her imagination can be stimulated by the customer's direct expression of the problem. The dynamics of such a customer encounter evoke far more creativity than does a memo you might write on the subject.

Finally, I wish to reemphasize the value of enhancing your existing products and expanding into new ones *within your existing customer base* to the extent possible before waltzing off into uncharted territory. Really understanding a market, developing deep and trusting relationships with the customers, and thoroughly knowing the relevant technologies are very long and costly processes whose value is usually grossly underestimated. However, if this effort yields an additional product within the same field, perhaps creating a *system,* marketing costs will be much lower and technical success will be far more likely than if you launch into a brand new field. Furthermore, this strategy builds greater barriers to competitors' developing a system of products.

Other sources of new or improved product ideas are:

- *Patent abstracts.* They may stimulate a fresh, yet-unpatented idea, or you may wish to negotiate a license with the patent holder.
- *Trade shows.* Looking at competitive or related products may trigger some new thoughts.

- *New product releases* in trade journals. These also may stimulate thinking. Often a new company will publish a release before it really gets underway, and hence is in the position where it may find acquisition or licensing of the product attractive.
- *Unsolicited proposals.* Every company inevitably gets an abundance of these, and most of them are inappropriate to the product plan. A very important word of caution: Be sure the procedure for reviewing these is done according to your legal counsel and that the submitter signs appropriate release forms before any potentially proprietary details are discussed. If this is not done, you may be liable if you later offer a similar product from an entirely different source.
- *Undirected time of your own technical people.* Try letting them spend 5% to 10% of their time on pursuits of their own liking and see what results.

In any event, remember there are very few breakthroughs or revolutionary products. The history of steam engine development started in 1680, and the concept of the computer can be traced to Charles Babbage over 100 years ago. Most products are enhancements of a predecessor or the transposition of technology from one product to another—which still can be a very creative act.

Creativity

We have been discussing the roles of disciplined thinking and intuitive leaps, so it is about time to delve more deeply into the issue of the creative process. I believe the work of the great scientist or the great product developer is very much the same as that of the great artist, in whom we see the manifestation of two powerful ingredients—the intuitive power that creates the vision and the physical skills to carry out that vision. From the artist's deepest unconscious comes the soul-stirring vision that cannot be seen by anyone else until those skilled hands wield the brush and paint in a way that conveys meaning to the same deep level in the viewer. Likewise, the great product designer, using a knowledge of science and the state of technology development, makes an intuitive leap into envisioning a product that resonates with the needs of the marketplace, and then with highly disciplined skill transforms this vision into the well-functioning physical product.

Most research into the creative process has, in one way or another, identified the following steps:

1. *Preparation.* This is the logical, disciplined accumulation of data, defining parameters, arraying alternatives, and struggling with weighting and valuing the factors. This step seems to be both a guide and stimulus to what follows.

2. *Incubation or "simmering."* Here the conscious preparation process is relaxed either intentionally or through fatigue. It may occur while taking a walk, drinking a glass of wine, staring out of the window, or sleeping.

3. *Illumination.* This is the moment of magic, when the entire solution may suddenly come to mind. It may bear no relationship to the earlier, consciously crafted alternative as it bursts forth from the deepest unconscious. It is accompanied by a feeling of exhilaration that can range from a pleasing little self-satisfying perk to what people have described as a "spiritual experience." If the task is forming a hypothesis to describe more deeply a principle of science, the intuitive experience may be as if the unconscious were in the presence of "those molecules." If it is toward designing a new product, the unconscious has brought together in a proper way some heretofore unrelated materials or designs, and it may feel like the perfection of the fit of that last piece of a jigsaw puzzle.

4. *Verification.* This is the testing of the idea, the attempt to translate it to a reality in the form of writing, drawing, prototype, or whatever form is appropriate.

Now let us look at some classical examples.

Mozart wrote of his experiences (as reported by William James):

First bits and crumbs of the piece come and gradually join together in my mind; then the soul getting warmed to the work, the thing grows more and more, and I spread it out broader and clearer, and at last it gets almost finished in my head, even when it is a long piece, so that I can see the whole of it at a single glance in my mind, as if it were a beautiful painting or a handsome human being; in which way I do not hear it in my

imagination at all as a succession—the way it must come later—
but all at once, as it were. It is a rare feast! All the inventing
and making goes on in me as in a beautiful strong dream. But
the best of all is the hearing of it all at once.[1]

Moving to the scientific field, the often described experience
of August Kekule telling of his discovery of the benzene ring (a
milestone in the progress of understanding organic chemistry) is
worth repeating here. While riding on a bus, he recounts,

I fell into a reverie, and lo, the atoms were gamboling before
my eyes! Whenever hitherto, these diminutive beings had ap-
peared to me, they had always been in motion; but up to that
time I had never been able to discern the nature of their motion.
Now, however, I saw how, frequently, two smaller atoms unite
to form a pair; how a larger one embraced the two smaller ones;
how still larger ones formed a chain, dragging the smaller ones
after them but only at the ends of the chain. I saw what our
past master Kopp, my highly honored teacher and friend, has
depicted with such charm in his *Molekular-Welt*; but I saw it long
before him. The cry of the conductor, 'Clapham Road', awak-
ened me from my dreaming; but I spent part of the night in
putting on paper at least sketches of these dream forms. This
was the origin of the 'Structural Theory'.[2]

In the same talk in Berlin in 1890 he stated:

It is said that a genius recognizes truth without knowing the
evidence for it. I do not doubt that even in ancient times this
kind of thinking occurred. Would Pythagoras have offered up
a hecatomb if he had recognized his famous theorem only after
finding a way to prove it?[3]

He concluded:

Let us learn to dream, gentlemen, then perhaps we shall learn
the truth.[4]

---

[1]William James, *The Principles of Psychology*, vol. 1 (New York: Dover Publications, 1950; reprinted by special arrangement with Henry Holt & Co.), p. 255.
[2]Ira Progoff, *Depth Psychology and Modern Man* (New York: McGraw-Hill), p. 217.
[3]*Ibid.*, p. 216.
[4]*Ibid.*, p. 219.

A Conceptual Framework of Creativity (and Innovation)

First I must say that this section is too brief for an adequate discussion of current psychological thought, and plummets far too quickly into psychological language for all to follow. If you are turned off by it, skip it and go to the next section on product design. If you are intrigued by it, get the book by Eric Neumann cited below, after reading some background on Jung.

The previous examples all suggest something in addition to the normal, rational, "controlled" way of functioning that we experience most of the time. Most aware people would acknowledge that unconscious forces play a key part in creativity, as most schools of psychology recognize the unconscious. The presence of a personal unconscious could be an adequate explanation of much of the "cleverness" we frequently display. Something we saw and forgot comes back to us—perhaps in a rearranged form—to present itself at the right time. This explanation is insufficient, however, to explain the experience described by Kekule or Mozart, or to explain the timeless works of art and literature, or even give adequate tribute to personal experiences many of us have had on rare creative occasions.

Here Jung's profound notion of the collective unconscious (discussed in Chapter 3), or objective psyche, with its archetypes clearly comes to the fore. In fact, one could reason in the other direction that truly significant creativity is evidence of the collective unconscious.

The collective unconscious differs from the personal (which encompasses the repressed data, images, and projections of one's personal experiences) in that it is not the result of personal experiences but is the inherited cumulative knowledge and experience of all human beings, available to each of us through its symbolic language. Underlying this region are the archetypes. These primordial imprints are activated by their particular stimuli and respond with a powerful energy manifested by symbols which influence our perception.

Now we start to have some language with which to conceptualize the creative process. Oversimplifying, a stimulus, intentional or otherwise, activates the archetype and from this comes imagery, which, if connected to the conscious process, forms the new thought or action. If this image arises from the depths of the collective unconscious the impact can be extraordinarily powerful—since it is of the same root as the most transcending of so-called spiritual experiences. If it comes from the shallower personal level, although energized by the archetypes, it may seem like a heady lift.

With this general framework in mind, one question immediately arises. Why, since we all have a collective unconscious with its archetypes, are we all not equally creative? The answer to this lies in defining the particular archetype that holds sway and its relationship to the ego, and is best described by Eric Neumann.

> The difference between the creative and normal man resides in an intensified psychic tension that is present in the creative man from the very start. In him a special animation of the unconscious and an equally strong emphasis on the ego and its development are demonstrable at an early stage . . . from childhood onward the creative individual is captivated by his experience of the unitary reality of childhood; he returns over and over again to the great hieroglyphic images of archetypical existence. They were mirrored for the first time in the well of childhood and there they remain until, recollecting, we bend over the rim of the well and rediscover them, forever unchanged . . . and because the dominance of the primary archetypical world is preserved and not replaced by that of the cultural canon, the development of personality and consciousness is subject to a different law than in normal man.[5]

The "unitary reality" with its "great hieroglyphic images" is the archetype of the Great Mother (not the actual mother) from which the creative person fails to be weaned. In "normal" development, the mythological images of the primordial Great Mother and Great Father are projected upon persons of the immediate family and, through this, the person adjusts to normal relationships with the community, or "cultural canon."

The path to outstanding creativity involves rejecting the Great Mother/Father in a step that frees the creative person from the confining, dominating aspects of the archetype. This allows them to live in a relationship with the archetype, having access to the imagery and symbols that "normal" people do not have. With a strong ego acting in tension with these symbolic resources, a transformation takes place—resulting in the creative act.

Jung's type definitions are worth noting as they relate to cre-

[5]Eric Neumann, *Art and the Creative Unconscious* (Princeton: Princeton University Press, 1974), pp. 180–181.

ativity. The *introvert,* who tends to perceive inner reactions more than the *extrovert's* attention to the outer world, may be more attuned to the forces of the unconscious. Four functions shape the creative process. *Intuition* provides a broad, ready grasp of the symbol or idea, *thinking* supplies the analysis, *sensation* relates it to reality, and *feeling* provides a measure of its human value. Thus we can see that a person in whom one function greatly predominates may have a shortcoming in the creative outcome. For example, a highly intuitive person may have trouble separating and apportioning value to the ideas.

Can Creativity Be Created?

Probably not to any significant degree. However, many attempts have been made—including brainstorming, the use of nature analogies (a suggestion of creativity's archetypical nature), right/left brain accessing techniques, and various other think-tank sessions. I believe the most that can be expected from these types of endeavors is a freeing or stimulation of the personal unconscious, allowing previously stored experiences to be jiggled around.

Jungian therapy, with its emphasis on accessing the unconscious and the transforming experiences of increased relationship between the ego and the unconscious, certainly works in the direction of enhanced creativity.

Skills training in writing, computer simulation, machining, and the like certainly can help someone bring an idea to reality.

Disciplined use of time and focusing of energies can add energy to the ego side of the tension-produced transformation process as well as help the implementation later needed.

In short, I believe certain steps can sharpen or hone clouded creative potential—but they cannot recreate the preponderance of the Great Mother archetype in the random person off the street.

Now Back to Some Suggestions on Product Design

First, let us summarize the ingredients of good product design as follows:

1. *Market knowledge.* Without this, the product will likely be functionally inappropriate.
2. *Latest knowledge of science and state of technology.* Without the

latest *appropriate* technology, the product will be technically inadequate or outdated.

3. *Intuitive vision.* Without this, the design will likely be overly complex, contrived, and evidencing "brute force" solutions. The product will not be admirable.

4. *Implementing skill.* Without this, functionality and certainly quality will be lacking.

A large number of compromises such as weight versus strength, or manufacturability versus a desired appearance rule every design. An inspired designer often uses these conflicts to create an entirely new solution. In contrast a compromise of the conflicting factors leaves both demands only partially satisfied. An example of this was the trend in airplane wing design in which low drag was achieved by smaller, thinner, more swept-back wings, which in turn compromised weight, fuel capacity, and the higher lift required for takeoff and landing. The compensating design included marvelously clever, complex folding high-lift devices which, while admirable in themselves, added to cost, maintenance, and weight. In other words, the compromises created a trend toward a design that strangled itself. Then along came Richard Whitcomb of NASA, who attacked the airfoil drag itself, resulting in a wing which could be thicker, less swept back, and longer (the now widely used super critical airfoil). Suddenly the wing became lighter, with more fuel capacity, requiring only simple lift augmentation devices which in turn are lighter and cheaper than the previous ones. By addressing the basic problem instead of cleverly designing compromises, the entire strangulation trend was reversed.

Another issue in product design is that of knowing when it is "right," before that all-critical evaluation by the marketplace. First, listen to your "innermost voice" as you review every detail. If it says "remember when that bearing surface stuck in the test but you said it would be OK in the production units?" *listen*, and take heed, for very likely it is the clue to a problem that will come back to haunt you two years from now. Second, pay attention to what your associates, friends, and children say. If your neighbor comes over and pushes the wrong button, let that be a clue to a potential problem. If your child says "that's crazy," at least think seriously about the possibility something is wrong.

The product of a gifted designer or design team can have an

inherent quality that transcends "meeting the specs" or may even go beyond precisely fitting the market need. This quality defies precise description but is characterized by simplicity of solutions, a creative directness that makes you gasp, thinking "why didn't someone think of that sooner," and an appropriateness to the function that includes benefits that market research would never think to ask and users would not know they needed.

Now for the sake of controversy I will mention a few products that I personally believe are of this stature. In autos, the Audi 5000 and Acura Legend were of this nature when they were introduced. In fasteners, cyanoacrylate (instant) glue, RTV[6] silicone, and Velcro[7] take prizes. In airplanes, the Boeing 727 (in the late 1960s and 1970s) and the Boeing 737–300 (for the current period of technology) both synchronized with their respective market needs. I would also include Ziploc Brand[8] bags, but none of the personal computers. Until they are roughly the size of an $8\frac{1}{2}"$ × 11" pad, with a screen of that size that has photographic resolution, and with most functions activated by voice input, they are certainly not "user friendly," in my terms.

Product Names and Logos

This is one area where endeavors in absurdity have reached startling heights as a result of insecure product people who believe there is magic in computer-selected names and graphic pun logos. While the computer dictionary can certainly remind us of syllables we have forgotten, and truly archetypical symbols can be extraordinarily powerful, most of what has been happening recently has been graphic pollution, with cutesy logos, tech-y word inventions, and insanity-producing acronyms.

While it is easy to criticize what is being done, it is not easy to come up with a good name for your product. One suggestion is that you listen to what everyone calls it, since a natural name may emerge that rings with easy-to-remember description. I will cite one example from my own experience at Raychem Corporation. When, many years ago, I was developing a type of wire termination consisting of a preform of solder inside a heat-shrinkable plastic tube, which would solder and insulate a connection in one

[6]Trademark of General Electric.
[7]Trademark of Velcro USA.
[8]Trademark of Dow Chemical.

heating step, we were struggling for a name. Many clever and cute tech-y names were thought of, but none seemed right.

Finally I reflected upon what people were already calling it—"solder sleeve"—and realized this homely, simple name was right. We christened it that, no one ever stumbled over it, and to this day it literally trips from the tongue when someone talks about this type of product—even for the first time.

As for logos, do not be too concerned about this little coat of arms. The likelihood you will leave an indelible image on our culture is remote indeed, and your time will be better spent talking to your customers.

Your Role in Marketing

First and foremost, *understand the technology in depth*. You cannot have the luxury of always "referring it to engineering" or "calling in my technical person" when you are trying to determine customer need or setting product direction. As we have discussed, the technical person should be vitally involved, but you also must know the technology (and the science behind it) to the "marrow of your bones."

Define and redefine current and future customer needs based upon the continual data gathering described in Chapter 4. The quality of the information is based upon the quality of your relationship with the customers.

Motivate the research, development, engineering, and manufacturing people by helping them establish a direct relationship with the customers.

Screen and select ideas generated by your technical people. Make the final decisions in consultation with technical, production, and financial people.

Guide the development of the selected products based upon customer needs.

Reward the efforts of the technical people by bringing them to visit the satisfied customer. While this may be one of the most powerful motivators of all, you also should tell these development people directly how pleased you are, pass the same word around the company, and of course tell their bosses, since it should have an effect upon salary and bonus reviews.

Catalyze the various resources of your company to bring the right talent to bear. For example, if a new opportunity requires chemical know-how and that is in another division, arrange to have the person with the needed knowledge present in your task-defining and creative sessions.

Your Plan

1. Recall a creative experience—one you feel proud of—and note the events leading up to it. What does it say about the creative process?
2. List a couple of products that are *so good* they seem to transcend what would be expected.
3. Decide if your product reflects
   a. market knowledge
   b. latest knowledge of science and technology
   c. intuitive vision
   d. implementing skill

8

Selling—The Art of It

S elling is one element of the marketing mix about which far too much has been written—much of it about "sure fire" techniques which, when fully mastered, can render the potential customer putty in your hands, the same as it does for the technique's "discoverer," Jack Headstrong, All American Salesman and World's Most Famous Lecturer. You perhaps have read a book or taken a course that, if we oversimplify, goes as follows:

> Get a new suit. Draw up your chin, pull in your stomach, and feel good about yourself. Call the customer with confidence and a sense of authority. Arrive on time and take charge of the interview. Keep the control. Sell benefits, not features. Cycle through your well-practiced series of ever-engulfing closes. Write the order and leave with a firm handshake. Pump yourself up again and repeat at the next customer.

Of course, this concept is woefully inadequate, is probably more detrimental than helpful, and certainly contributes heavily to the caricature of the salesperson as a slick blowhard.

While a newer form of "serve the customer" is coming into its own, I am going to take a different view—looking at what the salesperson must *do* and *be* to maximize the customer's "valuing image" and in turn its two components, the reality and the "projected" or fantasy as described in Chapter 3. These comments apply to any category of salesperson—direct factory, independent representative, or distributor.

What the salesperson must *do*, to do everything right, constitutes a base level of performance that is necessary for anyone and, if performed fully and well, will be categorized as "C" level performance.

What the salesperson must *be* will be further broken down into two categories: first, the ability to develop and sustain a relationship, and second, the ability to trigger and sustain the "projected" image or fantasy of the customer. "C" level performance plus ability to develop and sustain *relationship* will be categorized as "B" level performance, while the combination of "B" plus ability to trigger and sustain the *fantasy* is "A" level performance.

Doing Everything Right—Level C Performance

This section deals with the logical, consciously controlled, disciplined actions that *must* be practiced by any and all successful salespeople. These actions *must become so ingrained that they come naturally,* done within the particular personality of the salesperson. They are comparable to the functions that become second nature in driving a car—stopping at red lights, signaling turns, and so on.

The following description will be based upon one of the more difficult situations—opening a new territory for a new product—but it may serve as a checklist for *all* situations, including the opposite extreme of taking over an established territory for an established product. In other words, if the following recommendations are used as guidelines in the most common of situations, you will probably always perform them well.

Before You Start

You must have the right attitude toward customers. The *right* attitude is that they are human beings like yourself, trying to get through life by the only way they know, and have similar basic needs, fears, hopes and frustrations that you do. Your task is to form a partnership with them to creatively join your company's capabilities with their needs. The *wrong* attitude is that they are an object to be manipulated, overpowered, seduced or snowed.

Study, study, study your company's products and capabilities. Study in equal detail those of the competition. Always remember you must be a valuable technical *resource* for the customer—not just a conduit for questions and answers from the factory. For this you are not needed—the customer has a phone and could make direct contact with the factory.

Analyze What Is "Do-able"

A critical factor to remember always is that business-to-business sales usually require more than one sales call. Even known products such as resistors, fasteners, and commodity chemicals require the establishment of a relationship with a customer. Specially engineered products involve a design cycle. A threshold number of calls is needed for each sale, and anything short of this results in all previous time spent being simply wasted. Therefore, the first thing to do is to perform your own calculations based on the following example.

Felix ("Fingers") Gripbloch, a new salesperson for Union Robotics, contemplated his newly assigned territory— Michigan and Ohio. After two nights of severe heartburn and gas pains (he was at that time in San Francisco), he was able to plan his "do-able" strategy based upon the following data:

- Sales quota $2 mil of new
  (from his manager, based upon   business
  a share of company goals)
- Average number of calls   8
  to reach threshold
- Probability of success once   50%
  threshold is reached
- Average number of calls per day   3
- Number of available field days per   160
  year
  (Last four assumptions were based upon prior experience of old-time salespeople.)

Calculation:
  Number of active projects

$$\frac{160 \text{ days} \times 3 \text{ calls/day}}{8 \text{ calls per sale}} = 60 \text{ projects or accounts}$$

Since $2 million is expected in new business, and only 50% of the projects will succeed, the projects or customers must be an average of

$$\frac{2,000,000}{60 \times .50} = \$67,000 \text{ potential}$$

Obviously, each situation will vary dramatically. An established account may require only one or even no additional calls for a certain increase in business. Also, maintenance of existing business is going to take time, and should be accounted for in a more refined calculation. Hence, while such a calculation is far from precise, it gives one sufficient perspective to avoid the mistake of making two calls each on 300 customers of $5,000 potential, performed with great diligence and resulting in virtually no sales.

Learn the Territory Quickly

- Acquire directories from industry associations. Obtain Chamber of Commerce directories, and supplier directories such as the Thomas Register.
- Talk with salespeople of related but noncompeting companies. They typically will have empathy for your plight and will themselves need all the camaraderie they can get, so you will usually find them very helpful. They can be particularly helpful with the more subtle issues of who's who in the decision structure, the personality quirks, and so on.
- If you were preceded by someone in your territory, absorb everything they know. Also, *independently* evaluate the territory, because your predecessor inevitably had some blind spots and distorted perceptions.
- Based upon all the data you can collect, prioritize the accounts—including 10% to 25% more than your prior calculation indicated you can handle. This is to compensate for fall-outs.
- Start a file on each company. As times goes on you should collect their product literature, annual reports, organizational charts, trade articles, your call reports, gossip, conference technical articles, and names, names, names of the people.
- Locate each company on a map, look at routes and airline schedules, and determine how to travel there the fastest.
- Learn the location of restaurants, motels, and pay phones.

The Sales Call

Setting It Up

- *You* call. Do not have your secretary do this since it is your first opportunity to establish rapport—and you may learn a lot on the phone regarding the opportunity.
- Call the highest person you can reach who would be involved with your product. He or she is often easier to reach than your targeted person, and a referral downward helps in getting the key person's attention. Once you have met the "boss" you can call him or her in the future without making your key contacts feel you are going over their heads.
- Schedule your visits to start as early as possible, i.e., at 8:00 A.M., because it can make the difference between one and two calls in the morning. Do not believe the old rationalization that no on wants to be bothered before 9:00 or 9:30 A.M.

Preparation for the Call

- Review the company file.
- List the goals of the call. For example, on a new or prospective call, goals might be:

  Learning their product line and its relationship to your product.

  Meeting the key people in the decision-making process.
  Identifying an opportunity and getting a commitment to the first step.

- If a more mature situation, goals might include:

  Obtaining test results.
  Selling the new engineer just assigned to the project involving your product.

  Asking for the order.

- Pack your kit with *everything* you could possibly use for information and demonstration, including literature, test data, background information on your company, samples and equipment for an active demonstration if your product lends itself to that. Do *not*, in the interests of saving your strength, tell yourself that you can send it in later if necessary. You can, but you risk the chance of losing that one brief shining moment when the vice president stops by your contact's desk for a quick comment and you can grab three minutes.

In the Customer's Lobby

- Treat the receptionists with professional courtesy and respect. If they look bored and you must wait, show them your product and speak about your company. They will appreciate it and remember you next time.
- Read the visitor's register to see who your competitors or producers of related products are calling on.
- Read the company rag.
- Study product displays or literature.
- Check the graffiti in the restroom.

On the Way to Your Contact

- Treat the technician or secretary who comes to get you with the same respect you would the boss. Introduce yourself, and get his or her full name clearly. (People are flattered to hear their names.) If it seems appropriate, tell your escort about your product and say that you would like a chance to demonstrate it. At least give them a brochure.

In the Selling Situation

- At the very beginning, be sure you meet and acknowledge each person in the group.
- Make a clear statement of your purpose, explain your company, who you are, and any other relevant data.
- Present your material in a clear, spontaneous way, but *always* remember there is something more important than what you are saying—that is, what the *customer* has to say. After your general product introduction, ask about its relation to their needs, ask about their present practice, and if at any time you see a customer's lip quiver, stop and ask for comments. Again, after you finish, ask an open-ended question such as "How does any of this relate to things you may be doing?"
- If a new person enters during the meeting—even if to only speak to one of your attendees—stop, and introduce yourself. The visitor may turn out to be the department head, and this

courtesy may mean the difference between staying for your meeting or immediately leaving, without your even knowing who it was.

- In the dialog following your presentation, ask, ask, ask technical questions until you truly understand the application. Think, "Does this all make sense?" If not, ask some more questions. Be sure you understand their *real* needs as well as their *perceived* ones.

- In a polite way, at the end of the meeting (best done privately to the ranking person in the group) ask if it is possible to see the equipment or factory area where your product will be used. Usually people will be pleased to show you. When in the area, introduce yourself to any workers you come in contact with, and perhaps give them your card or a brochure. They are rarely treated this way, and you can be sure this symbol of respect will serve you well when they are struggling with the first problem using your product after your sale. Ask them about problems with their current products or materials.

As the Project Moves Along

- Sense the cycle and rhythm of the relationship. It is like making love—every person in every situation has a natural rhythm, and unless the partner can sense this and tune into it the results are less than optimum. The buying situation is the same, and the interest levels or attention span of the customer may have little to do with the actual timing of the project. Pay attention to the "breathing" of the customer rather than the scheduling chart on the wall.

- Check and cross-check how the decisions are made to be sure you are spending time the right way. Do so by asking, "Let me see now—once you have approved it, where does it go?"

- Keep *all* parties even remotely related fully informed and sold. For example, if you are quite sure your key specifier is the manufacturing engineer, continue to keep up your good work on purchasing, design engineering, and production management. In other words, sell the people that could potentially *block* the sale, not just the ones that can *push* it.

- Keep your entrepreneurial vision alert. Split your focus— while keeping one eye on the project, be constantly looking for the unexpected. The unexpected is often where the great new opportunity presents itself. If your contact mentions a big problem, ask about it. If you hear that some project got held up, find out why. It may be an opportunity ten times the size of what you are doing.

- Be sure any "inside" salesperson who is championing your product is thought well of. Occasionally someone on the losing side will pick up on a program in desperation. Be aware of the tone of voice of others as the name is mentioned, and observe interactions in meetings, or simply ask someone else, "Is Gerald Putzwell seen as the focal point for this decision?"

- If a project is worth pursuing, never finish without a commitment to action. This may be a customer agreeing to try something or your agreeing to run some tests or bring them something—but be sure there is something. Otherwise, things die and you have no excuse to go back in.

- Throughout the cycle, continue to furnish "rationalization" aids such as lab reports, comparative tests and costs, tests to agency specifications, and anything else that will help this "logical" process run its course so the buyer can feel comfortable with the earlier subconscious decision.

- Whenever you mention other customers, *always* be sure you have their permission, and *state* this as a preface to mentioning them. This way your customer of the moment will feel confident you are not spreading around their data.

And Finally—The Purchase Order

- When the time seems ripe, ask for the order, directly and simply. For instance, "Now that this has proven out on the tests and experiments (or on the production line), what quantity do you plan to requisition? I would suggest 10,000 or more because of the better price break." Here is perhaps the greatest challenge and one in which your own ingenuity must really come to the front. The important thing is that you do ask for the order.

- When the big deal is about to come through, consider yourself an obstetrician delivering a baby, and treat the situation with comparable concentration. You should never allow your attention to flag, even briefly. This means daily or hourly visits or phone calls until the order is tightly in hand.

- If the product requires any customer training, do it with the same care (down to the last worker who will come within ten feet of it) as you did selling it.
- Follow through *impeccably* on *all* commitments.
- Work *very, very* hard.

Entertainment

A meal, whether it is lunch or dinner, can help wherever it is timely and appropriate. Conventional views hold that this setting provides an easy place to talk, a chance to get to know the buyer better, and maybe, just maybe, creates a slight feeling of obligation in the mind of the buyer. While much of this is probably true, the psychological significance and implications of sharing a meal go much deeper. In states of tension, people revert to eating. If you don't believe this, ask your friends to tell you about their recent trip abroad—even to the most worldly a slightly tension-inducing experience. Will you get a response regarding the cultural discoveries, the current political situation, or the theater? No—you will first hear about some "great restaurant." In fact you may get such a complete five-course perspective from the gastrointestinal tract that you wish you had never asked. Moving from states of tension to those of pleasure and celebration, the "breaking of bread" together has had special significance in most cultures throughout history—suggesting an archetypical ingredient.

From a practical point of view a timely big forkful, coupled with etiquette's rule about not talking with your mouth full, can give you an opportunity for reflective thought in a negotiating discussion. Furthermore, since etiquette requires all people to finish the meal at the same time, the accompanying conversation provides a subtle exercise in cooperation.

With these thoughts in mind, take your customers to lunch or dinner, observing the two following rules.

- Do it appropriately and comfortably. Suggesting a gourmet dinner after the first call may be awkward if not downright embarrassing. A tasty lunch after the third successful visit, assuming you both have something to talk about, can be quite enhancing.
- Choose a place where the tastes and quality are outstanding though not necessarily expensive. Even those who appear to

have only a large gullet and no palate can develop the latter. Tastes (along with smells) linger in our memories in a very pervasive way—and an outstanding veal à la creme may remain associated with your product a lot longer than your eloquent product presentation.

Regarding other forms of entertainment, such as a ball game, the theater, a ski trip, or tennis, other rules should prevail:

- The invitation should never put a person in an uncomfortable or compromised situation. If government employees or people working for certain companies have entertainment restrictions, do not put them in the position of having to decline.
- It should be a natural outgrowth of a mutual interest—suggested at a time when the relationship has evolved to that point.
- The activity should not involve expenditures that in any way can be seen as enough to impose an obligation. In addition to its unethical and in some cases illegal dimension, such an experience creates a nagging sense of discomfort in the recipient—no matter how enjoyable it might be. This will sooner or later result in a "pulling back" in the business relationship.

In short, these instructions for Level C performance describe a job well done but without necessarily much human relationship. From the discussion of buying decisions in Chapter 3, this performance fulfills that portion of "reality" based on the *actions* of the salesperson. If the customer were asked to describe this salesperson, we might hear, "I don't know her very well, but she seems O.K. However, she sure does a great job for me; she knows her stuff and I can depend on her doing what she says."

In short, this is *functioning* well and is base-level performance necessary from any salesperson, hence, it is termed "C."

Doing Everything Right, Plus Relationship—Level B Performance

The Nature of Relationship

A sales situation is much more likely to be successful—and, more important, be sustained—if there is a sense of relationship be-

tween the salesperson and buyer. A somewhat elusive term to
define, yet one we all understand, relationship suggests liking, a
feeling of trust and mutual enhancement. It does not necessarily
mean close social or personal interactions, but rather the feeling
the customer might express as "I like to see him come by. I like
him, I trust him, I feel good when I'm with him, I learn something, and he always comes through for me". The key ingredient
of relationship is authenticity, and this characteristic on the
salesperson's part stems from a strong sense of self, sincerity, integrity and a realistic view of one's role in the world. It must
include a sincere interest and belief in the company and its products. From an inner nature, the salesperson must feel a *respect and
interest in the customer as a person*—not as a money machine to be
manipulated.

How do we define authenticity? The passages that follow may
help.

Whenever a feeling is voiced with truth and frankness, whenever a deed is the clear expression of sentiment, a mysterious
and far-reaching influence is exerted. At first it acts on those
who are inwardly receptive. But the circle grows larger and
larger. The root of all influence lies in one's own inner being:
given time and vigorous expression in word and deed, its effect
is great. The effect is but the reflection of something that ema-
nates from one's own heart.[1]

And a much better known one—

Go placidly amid the noise and haste, and remember what
peace there may be in silence. As far as possible without surren-
der be on good terms with all persons. Speak your truth quietly
and clearly, and listen to others, even the dull and ignorant;
they too have their story. Avoid loud and aggressive persons;
they are vexatious to the spirit. If you compare yourself with
others, you may become vain and bitter; for always there will
be greater and lesser persons than yourself. Enjoy your
achievements as well as your plans. Keep interested in your
own career, however humble; it is a real possession in the
changing fortunes of time. Exercise caution in your business
affairs for the world is full of trickery. But let this not blind you

[1]*The Book of Changes*, Bollingen Series XIX, translated by Richard Wilhelm, ren-
dered into English by Cary F. Baynes (Princeton: Princeton University Press,
1967).

to what virtue there is; many persons strive for high ideals, and everywhere life is full of heroism. Be yourself. Especially, do not feign affection. Neither be cynical about love; for in the face of all aridity and disenchantment it is perennial as the grass. Take kindly to counsel of the years, gracefully surrendering the things of youth. Nurture strength of spirit to shield you in sudden misfortune. But do not distress yourself with imaginings. Many fears are born of fatigue and loneliness. Beyond a wholesome discipline, be gentle with yourself. You are a child of the universe, no less than the trees and the stars; you have a right to be here. And whether or not it is clear to you, no doubt the universe is unfolding as it should. Therefore be at peace with God, whatever you conceive Him to be, and whatever your labors and aspirations, in the noisy confusion of life keep peace with your soul. With all its sham, drudgery and broken dreams it is still a beautiful world. Be cheerful. Strive to be happy.

—"Desiderata" by Max Ehrmann[2]

To summarize, if you want to build solid relationships, based on the admiration of your customers, be on the track toward "getting your own self together first!"

Rapport

Personal authenticity must be communicated to the buyer to establish relationship, and this is where rapport comes in. Rapport is more than providing information (which one can do in a letter). It is a verbal and body language resonance between people. It is a flow of exchanges, including agreements, agreements about disagreements, laughs, implied understandings, shared feelings, acknowledgements, and reinforcements. It gets the "juices flowing," with each person feeling unconditionally accepted and understood. The process *must* be based on the salesperson having a *genuine* interest in the customer as a person. If it is forced, either it will seem phony to the customer or the salesperson will slip out of the script in a moment of carelessness, causing the customer to feel manipulated and betrayed.

In the resonance of rapport, active listening and contagious enthusiasm are key elements. More energy is generated by feelings than facts. The nature of questions and responses must be predicated on the personality type of the other person. For example, a careful, detailed, step-by-step thinking person may not like the quick swipe responses characteristic of people who like to talk in "shorthand."

Perhaps the best attitude for the salesperson to take in establishing rapport with a customer is to feel that the person is someone with whom you are simply trying to have an interesting conversation. Get out of the role of being a salesperson trying to do something to someone, but imagine instead you are trying to develop an acquaintance with your new neighbor.

A reasonable level of ability to develop rapport is necessary for authentic relationships to be established and hence "B" level selling to occur. However, to perform at the "A" level, to be described next, requires *extraordinary* rapport.

Doing Everything Right, Plus Relationship, Plus Magic—Level A Performance

To a varying degree in all purchases, the buyer has a dream, one that stems from the forces of the unconscious described in Chapter 3. It can be a mild dream where the selection of office notepads is reinforced by the buyer's personal unconscious connecting that style of paper to the one used for his or her praised high school essay. It can be a powerful fantasy, stemming from the deep collective unconscious such as "I'm finally going to be known as someone who makes changes around here by throwing out IBM and installing Rutabaga components" (the hero archetype at work).

In truly great selling, "B" level performance is combined with the *ability to keep the powerful energies of these unconscious driven fantasies from burning out as quickly as they normally would*. This constitutes the "A" level. It occurs when the salesperson intuitively perceives and instinctively responds to the customer's unconsciously driven energies and images (the positive ones) so sensitively that they are enhanced and further magnified. It is rapport practiced at the level of art. It can be felt, only partially described, and not prescribed. We have all felt "being on a roll" with someone. "With him I can really be myself, and I feel greater than at any other time." "I feel really good with her because she knows me."

In the mystery of its nature, one ingredient may be evident—that is, the buyers feel so listened to and so approved of by someone they trust that they are free to continue to "dream the impossible dream."

Considerations

Obviously, there is no sharp dividing line between the "B" and "A" levels—rather "A" is the extended area of a continuum. However, for sake of identifying and discussing the traits, I have chosen to separate them. Both involve intuitively knowing when the unconscious decision is made and what the flow of the energy curve looks like at any time—hence, knowing its second peak, or the time to close the sale.

The best salespeople cannot perform at "A" level in all situations, and even the worst will probably function at "A" level at certain times with certain people. Hence, the distinction is somewhat situational. The overall evaluation of salespeople must be based on the extent and frequency with which they function at the higher levels. A fairly consistent "B" level with occasional "A" situations means a "damn good" salesperson for the business-to-business environment where long-term relationships are key. A sales force of such people is a powerhouse.

The ability to release the customer's fantasy but not to establish relationship is not at all uncommon among salespeople. These are the instant "charmers" who may have, or may not have, authenticity to back it up. They also may be much better at releasing the buyer's fantasy than sustaining it. If these people also have "C" level skills, they can be effective in "one time" sales situations—more typically those with consumer products such as autos, insurance, and real estate.

Chapter 15 discusses how to select and train a sales force for the highest overall performance levels. A responsive, disciplined person with a reasonably good personality can be trained to do "C" level performance. "B" level depends more on the person's makeup, although skills training in listening may help a little. "A" level cannot be taught, and the indication of whether or not sales candidates have it is how much in the grip of their personality you and your associates feel at the end of an interview. Are you feeling so good about yourself in their presence that you do not want to let them leave?

Your Plan

1. We each buy things every day. List those characteristics in the person with whom you are dealing that increase your likelihood of purchasing.
2. List your characteristics that you would exercise as a salesperson (i.e., technical skill, empathetic listening, sex appeal, courtly manners, cache of awful jokes, spontaneous wit, loud voice, new shoes, etc. etc.).
3. Draft the story you would typically tell to sell your product.
4. Picture yourself as a salesperson. Based upon your assessments of your characteristics, in what percentage of the situations would you be functioning at each level?

A _____%

B _____%

C _____%

9

Selling— The Structure of It

S hould you hire your own salespeople, use reps, depend upon distributor salespeople, or all of the above? This is the question facing anyone marketing a technical or business-to-business product, unless the strategy is strictly direct mail. It is an obvious question with a new company or new product, but may emerge again later. For example, a new company may start with reps, then at a sales volume of $3 to $10 million will start to consider converting to their own salespeople. This chapter addresses this overall question in order to put the selling job in its proper perspective in the marketing mix.

So there will be no confusion of terms, selling is *direct* verbal interaction with the customer, either in person or by phone, with the goal being the sale of the product. It is not advertising, promotion, or other elements of the marketing mix. In addition to the interaction with the customer, it may include "selling" to the distributors.

Alternatives

As mentioned above, the choices are company-employed salespeople, independent representatives (reps), distributor salespeople (if distribution is used), or a combination thereof.

Company salespeople are, as the name implies, simply employees of the company.

Reps are independent sales agents, usually working on commission only, typically representing six to twenty related but non-competing product lines in a designated territory. Unlike distributors, they do not take title to the product but are simply part-time salespeople working for 5% to 15% of the sales price if they succeed in making the sale.

Distributor salespeople are the ''feet on the street'' of the ''storehouse.''

Distributors purchase your product for resale (take title to it). They are discussed in Chapter 10, but it should be stated here too that distributor salespeople are part of the equation only if independent distributors are an appropriate part of the marketing mix. In other words, you would not consider them an alternative to reps or your own people if distribution is not needed.

Factory Salespeople Versus Independent Representatives

The most important consideration is *what does it take to do the required job?* To examine this, let us break down the job.

Technical Competency and Knowledge.

This is the most important factor of all, and if this is not present, all the other factors become irrelevant. If the product is complex and its application requires solid scientific background, the *company person wins every time.* First of all, you select each and every one of your own people. You train them and control them. You have no voice in who a rep firm hires (other than changing firms). Even if a particular rep is a true expert (a key design engineer in the product before going into the rep business), this is only one person out of several in the firm. Even more important, this rep must keep up on a number of other lines. This cannot compare to someone who lives and breathes your product only—its nuances, the complexity of application, and so on—eight to twelve hours a day.

In general, if a product is fairly standard, the entire story can be clearly described in a four-page brochure, and specification sheets and price lists answer most of the questions, a good technically educated rep may be able to handle it. I should stress the point of technical education. There tends to be a world of difference between people grounded in science and non-technically trained people (exposed to the same specific product training) in their skill in responding to problems, new applications, or any out-of-the-ordinary situations.

Whom the Customer Needs, Wants, and Expects

A rep can sell a supply of voltmeters to a purchasing agent or even work with the engineer to get them specified. The customer can feel completely well taken care of and satisfied by this transaction. In fact, the customer probably knows the rep from other product lines represented and may well have developed a friendship over the years.

Now, if that rep tried to sell a large computer installation or a custom-designed robotic assembly system, the vice president or even the president involved in the final decision would probably think it quite unusual and would balk at paying a rep commission on the price when all the work was done by factory engineers. The customer's technical people would find the role of the rep superfluous—other than paying for lunch. So even though the rep might be technically competent and liked by the customer, he or she would not be seen by the customer as appropriate to the situation.

In short, understand the view the customer has of what it takes to do the job.

Dollar Size of the Unit Sale

If the average annual purchase of a customer is $10,000 a year and it requires four sales calls (factored by .50 probability of success), the factory salesperson cost might be calculated as follows:

$$\frac{\text{Salesperson cost / year} = \$100,000}{\text{No. of sales calls} = 160 \text{ days} \times 3 \text{ calls/day}} = \text{approx. } \$200/\text{sales call}$$

$$8 \text{ calls} = \frac{4 \text{ needed}}{.5 \text{ probability}} = \frac{\$1,600}{\$10,000} = 16\% \text{ of sales dollars}$$

A rep commission would likely be 5% to 10%, so the choice would seem to favor reps. However, the decision must be overlaid with the question "Can the sale be made by the rep?" If the product is too technical, or for any other reason the sale cannot be successfully handled by the rep, it is not a bargain *at any price.*

You would be better off accepting the 16% sales cost, but at least *getting the order* (assuming it is still profitable, of course).

Gestation Time to Sale

The shorter the time the more the rep is motivated. Programs that require a two- to four-year design-in cycle are not a big turn-on to reps, who may figure you will drop them before the payoff ever happens.

Number and Concentration of Customers

In a widely dispersed customer base of many small to medium-sized customers, it is easy to reason that coverage is more readily obtained by reps. With their other lines, they can afford to have enough people to get someone out to Joplin, Missouri to see those two potential customers. This can be true, but the issue warrants careful study. Reps require a lot of support, as will be described later in the chapter, and you must estimate the support costs versus the incremental business from these rural accounts. Furthermore, it takes time to get the 50 or so people (10 rep firms × 5 people each) to change their thinking patterns to incorporate your product in a productive way.

   If the product is new, and/or complex, you can fall into a trap by concentrating first on setting up a national rep organization. Much of your time will be consumed in administrating, training, and attempting to direct the rep activity, and all you will have as a result for a considerable period of time is a very well dispersed but marginally effective selling effort. In many situations I believe *three* "commandos," i.e., factory sales engineers with depth of knowledge, boundless energy, authority to make commitments, and an unrestricted air travel card, can introduce a product faster, with more immediate sales, than *fifty* floundering reps. This is particularly true if the typical pattern prevails that fewer than thirty customers constitute over 50% of the potential business.

Making the Decision

By now it might appear to you that I am biased toward a direct sales force. You are right. If your plan is to grow to be a significant factor in your marketplace, if the product is quite technical, if you expect the technology to evolve rapidly, and if you depend upon customer feedback to trigger and guide this innovation, then direct sales in the *only* way to go.

If the realities are such you simply are not funded sufficiently to start this way, I would suggest the following: First go back to your funding source—venture capital or corporate moneybags—and plead the case. If this fails, attempt a modified approach such as hiring one, two, or three direct people to launch the introduction to the key customers. Then proceed with a mixture of additional company people as they can be afforded for key territories, coupled with reps for the less concentrated territories.

At the other end of the spectrum, a rep organization can be quite appropriate if most of the following conditions are present.

- Product is fairly "standard" with the sales story reducible to a four-page brochure.
- Constant and dramatic new product developments are *not* part of the scene.
- Customer base is widely dispersed and few territories will grow rapidly to the volume that would support a full-time person.

Additional Issues

Two things should be mentioned at this point regarding the nature of the selling effort.

First, if you are introducing a new product which is the specific creation of one or several inventors, involve them in the sales effort. They will gain invaluable feedback and, unless they are personality disasters—which is quite rare—their infectious enthusiasm can carry the sales encounter a long way.

Second, I must address the new hype term *telemarketing*, touted as though it were an alternative selling method.

Telemarketing is a term with which I have a lot of trouble. If it means simply calling up a customer or potential customer to introduce your company and determine what interest there may be in your product, follow up on inquiries, check the progress of a test, or even to see if a prospective customer is yet in position to place an order—then it is doing just what you should be doing naturally—without any phony (pun intended) labels.

If it means hiring a motormouth, providing a script and the phone book and instructions to sell "free" encyclopedia trials, then the term and the process deserve each other.

Primarily, I am concerned that the hyping of "telemarketing" suggests it is an alternative selling strategy, which it is not. In any type of selling, you naturally use the phone where appropriate. It is cheaper and quicker than a personal visit where it can serve the purpose, but does not deserve any contrived conceptualization such as "telemarketing." It is just being sensible—despite what the telephone company and a few intellectually bankrupt consultants would like you to believe.

The remainder of the chapter will be devoted to reps, since distributors are covered in Chapter 10 and direct selling people in Chapter 15.

If You Choose Reps

How to Find the Right Ones

The first source should be your key potential customers. As entrepreneur, product manager, or marketing manager, the most vital thing you do in *learning your market* is to talk with the key customers. In this discussion, ask them to name two or three rep firms that would seem suited for this type of product.

Other good sources are the firms successfully using reps for similar but noncompeting lines. For example, if you are developing a line of electrical capacitors, find out who represents the better resistor companies in the area, and ask the national sales managers of those companies about their reps.

Trade association meetings are another good source since you can observe the way reps interact.

Finally, advertising in trade journals or exhibiting at a trade show is going to bring out hungry reps—including a number you want to avoid, such as poor performers who always need new lines because they are constantly being dropped, and "alligator mouths" who take on more lines than they can handle hoping to pick off a few windfalls from each.

On the other hand, a very good possibility may be lurking among the hungry; that is the new person of excellent capability who is just starting in the rep business. Your line can be quite preoccupying to such an individual, "imprinting" them sufficiently so that you get a disproportionally high amount of their time.

Do not be overly impressed with reps' claims of contacts, relationships, "owning" an account, and the like. In almost any industrial situation, the right person can be located within three phone calls and, if you have a good product, a "relationship" can develop on the first visit.

How to Decide If They Are the Right Ones

The following endorsements are highly desirable:

- Two or three of the key customers should speak well of them.
- Several of the companies they represent, and even more important *formerly* represented, should think highly of them.
- Your own "gut feeling" should strongly favor them. You should feel they would be suitable to hire as your own salespeople.

In addition there are several "objective" requirements:

- Being technically trained and knowledgeable in your industry. In the interview, see how technically curious they are.
- Calling on your targeted accounts already, with compatible but noncompeting products.
- Covering the required geographical territory.
- Being staffed sufficiently, and financed properly to represent you well.

The Agreement

The written agreement should be prepared by an experienced lawyer and signed by both parties, and should cover at least the following issues.

- *Products to be handled.* If your company has multiple product lines, the particular lines involved should be clearly distinguished from the others. State whether you expect reps to handle "special" or nonstandard applications.
- *Geographical territory.*
- *Customer segment.* In certain situations you may wish to exclude certain types or specific accounts for direct attention by

company sales engineers. If there is any question regarding customers or products, do not include them. It is easier to add later than to take away.

- *Exclusivity and noncompetition.* For a given territory, the rep should be given exclusive rights and in turn should agree not to handle competing lines.
- *Commissions.* The rate should be at least average to slightly on the high side for your particular industry and product. This usually ranges from 5% for components that are likely to result in continuous business to 25% for lower priced one-time purchased instruments. Rates must be addressed for the following situations if applicable:

  - *Specials* or customer-engineered products where most of the selling is done by the manufacturer but later servicing is by the rep. This might bear anything from one-half to full rate.
  - *Existing accounts.* These may be commissioned from one-half to full.
  - *Split territories,* where the initial approval is achieved in one territory but delivery and subsequent follow-up are done at another plant in another rep's territory. These may be individually negotiated, but a 50/50 split may be a good starting point to put into the contract.

  Commissions are typically paid within ten days or at the end of the month during which payment from the customer is received.
- *Plant visits.* Reps should agree to visit the factory or attend a sales meeting once a year, at their travel expense.
- *Reports.* The rep should agree to keep the manufacturer apprised of the status of projects and names of customer contacts.
- *Authority of rep.* The agreement should state whether or not the rep may, without specific approval of the factory, quote price, deliveries, discounts, approve credit, or accept rejects. In general, it is best to delegate as much as the specific situation allows since doing so provides better response to the customer.
- *Termination.* Typically this requires 30 to 60 days notice by either party. Furthermore, the first 60 days should be considered a trial period with no obligations if termination occurs

within this period. After this period, continuation of commissions beyond the date of termination must be addressed.
Since lead times vary greatly between industries, a fixed period from termination may be difficult to establish fairly. One
starting point might be that on accounts where the rep did
effectively get your product specified, a commission would
be paid for one year beyond the date of the first order.

How to Make the Marriage Work

First and foremost, train your reps thoroughly in your products—
preferably at your plant so they develop a feeling of *knowing* as
opposed to *knowing about* your company. Relationships that are
started on a face-to-face basis make later telephone dealings function at a better level. Cover their on-site expenses, but let them
pay their own plane fares so they have an investment in the
process.

Continue training. On your travels, frequently hold training
seminars at their offices (5 to 7 P.M. with refreshments—maybe
followed by your paying for dinner). This covers other sales
people and office staff who have not visited the plant. Have samples and maybe a video showing the facilities, latest product developments, and—most important—the people about whom they
hear or with whom they deal on the phone.

Travel to the customers with them. Make sure they carry the
ball in the sales presentation; don't succumb to their pressure
to introduce you as the expert, casting you into the role of the
salesperson. This does two things—it provides an opportunity to
observe their style and product knowledge, and makes them involved and committed to follow on with the customer.

Support, support; respond, respond. Provide reps with all the
sales aids they reasonably need—plenty of clear literature, lucid
technical descriptions, checklists of sales points, samples or demonstration aids, and clear pricing and delivery data. When they
call for information or help, respond immediately. If the answer
cannot be given at that time (e.g., tests are not complete), tell
them when to expect it and then follow through impeccably.

Be consistently *tough* in demanding that goals be set and met,
that customers are serviced thoroughly and your company is represented in the manner you wish. For example, with leads you
refer to them, demand a report on follow-up. On the other hand,

be *generous* and rewarding for excellent performance. This certainly should be in the form of verbal praise, but also can take the form of bonuses, trips, or other perks.

Remember the following things that are guaranteed to turn off a rep:

- Slow response (or no response at all) to phone calls or written messages.
- Insufficient or confusing data regarding either the product or sales expectations.
- Late quotes.
- The impression that you are not living up to the spirit of the contract in some way.
- Feeling that you do not really care about them or what they do.

If You Must Divorce

Do so *decisively* if it is necessary due to inadequate or improper performance. However, do so as gracefully as possible, since reps will be continuing to call on your customers with other products. "Bad mouthing" is something you do not need. One example of "grace" is to pay their commission for a period appropriate to the effort (maybe longer than the agreement) in those areas where they actually did something well. In short, be tough but more than fair.

What Life with Reps Is Really Like

Out of ten carefully chosen reps, two will be great. They will be entrepreneurs in the finest sense, with outstanding sales ability and the technical knowledge to handle the product adequately. Their attention to your product line will never fail to please you, and you will be happy to have them represent your company.

Two will probably fail because you simply cannot get their attention. Although they met all your criteria, their selling patterns will be too fixed to incorporate your product.

Six will be roller coasters of satisfactions and frustrations. In one instance you will be ready to make a replacement because of inactivity until they improbably land a good order. In another your visit and pep talk will produce results for six weeks, and then it is back to never hearing from them. In still another case, they have just hired two new people to cover key accounts neither of whom possesses the technical expertise to understand your product. Another gets you the sales but the white shoes and pale green sports coat with matching tie make you grind your teeth when jointly visiting a customer.

If you still might like more detail, read on for a rather disgusting and sexist description.

Rep firms are typically founded by an ornery salesman in midlife crisis. Depending upon whether he internalizes or externalizes his ego problems, he may name the firm "Gerald Ohm and Associates" or "Trans Hyperdynamics International, Ltd."

Gerald drives a Mercedes and the salespeople full-size Chevys traded every two years. The office is in a new business development section near the airport. Gerald has a large office, large polished wooden desk, and trophies— tennis from his pre-40-year-old days and golf for the more recent endeavors. On the wall is a large map of the territory, marked off by sales regions. Gerald identifies the regions by salespersons' names (he sees himself as a people person) as well as numbers (01 thru 05) for the newly installed computer. On the map are colored pins having something to do with key accounts.

It will be immediately apparent that the office is run by Helen, the founder's secretary, who is 36, divorced, very shapely, fairly attractive, and totally loyal to Gerald. She is assisted by a 23-year-old named Jill who is very attractive, but nearly totally incompetent. Each of the salesmen suspects most of the others have "made it" with her, but even their ribbing each other about it does not produce solid enough responses so anyone can be sure. In any event, they are not going to complain to the boss about her work yet.

When you first made contact with Gerald Ohm about handling your product line he told you, "I rarely seek new lines to represent since I have a well established number of principals and am constantly being approached by companies wanting me to represent them." He then went on to say, "However, I am particularly impressed with your product, and in fact had two major companies ask me last week if we carried something like it. (In interviews with fifteen rep organizations you heard this same line ten times.)

Reps are repositories (maybe that is the source of the abbreviation) of bad jokes, including memorizing and relating details ad nauseam. (If only the memory capacity required for this could be used to store the specifications of your products instead!) They seem to be operating under the assumption that these tales, which perhaps caused knee-whomping in Toledo fifteen years ago, relax a customer over lunch, failing to see the stress the poor client goes through to cough up the expected guffaw.

Reps absolutely insist on paying for breakfast when they travel with you. This automatically puts you in the position of paying for lunch or dinner, and one arcane specialization of all reps is expensive restaurants.

However, an area in which all reps merit total admiration is their uncanny ability to have only *your* samples and *your* literature in their cars, *your* correspondence on their desks, and urgent phone calls from companies wanting *your* products when you are visiting them—even if you arrive unexpectedly and even though you have not heard a thing from them for four weeks. *Note to reps reading this:* I realize that this gross exaggeration does not apply to *you*—only to your competitors—but I do hope it suggests an opportunity.

Manufacturers who need reps in their strategy are desperate for rep firms with salespeople who can properly represent their products and company. This means salespeople with intelligence, education, integrity, and energy. It means a firm that does not take on more lines than it can handle with sufficient attention. It means firms that function as though they are actually employees of the manufacturers.

Your Plan

1. Direct or reps?
2. How many?
3. Where?
4. What qualifications?
5. What do you expect from them?
6. Training needed?

10

Distributors

With distribution costing 15% to 50% of the price of a product, the question of when and how to use distributors becomes vital. This chapter tells you what they are, when you need them, how to choose them, and how to work with them to insure they play their proper role.

What Are Distributors?

Stocking-Only Distributors

They are *stores* for customers in the local area. In case you have never seen one, I offer the following description.

> If an electronics distributor, it is located in a ten-year-old industrial park in one of the plastic-molded buildings alongside the electronics manufacturing companies. If a hydraulic fittings distributor, it will be in a forty-year-old building down by the tracks next to the steel supply distributor. If a medical products distributor, it will be located halfway between.
>
> The founder and president, a towering man, with a name like James Olsen, arrives every morning at 7:30 and parks his Cadillac in the space marked "President." He still closes the larger annual contracts, if the meeting does not interfere with his Wednesday golf afternoon.
>
> The front quarter of the building consists of Mr. Olsen's spacious, trophy-filled office and an open area with a num-

ber of desks where the "inside" salespeople hold forth continuously on the phone. Among them is likeable Ron (every
distributor has a likeable Ron), who is 29, unmarried but has
a steady girlfriend, and drives a yellow Camaro. People
like Ron develop outstanding telephone relationships with
purchasing agents whom they may never personally meet,
around products neither may understand, and based upon
inane conversations neither may recognize as inane.

Joe (purchasing agent): "Ron, how ya doin' ol' buddy?
Gotta get some of those P4–73926–482's. Got twenty dozen
in stock? I don't know what the hell they are, but got to
have them by Wednesday!"

Ron: "Just a minute, Joe—let me see if it's in the computer.[1] We sure have, Joe. Our truck will deliver them
Wednesday morning. Thank you, Joe. How's things at Hy-
pertech?"

Joe: "Great! How's things with you?"

Ron: "Great! Anything else we can do? We just took on
the Intercontinental Hydraulic Tech Ltd. line."

Joe: "Great, Ron! Send some literature. I don't know
what they do, but I'll keep it on file."

Ron: "O.K.—See you, Joe."

Joe: "Thanks, Ron. See you."

Then there is the "Will Call." Manning this typical store
counter (every distributor has one, usually located around to
the side with a small sign marked with the quaintly optimis-
tic phrase, "will call") are one or two clerks with personalities quite unsuited to deal with the customers. In this situation, if you can first find it, and then tolerate it, you can
actually walk in and buy something.

Next are the "outside" salespeople. These are the princes
and princesses, youngish men in three-piece suits, with
premature beer pots and blow-dried haircuts; older grey
foxes; and perky women (in electronics and medical, probably not in hydraulics) first hired as tokens, but then it was
discovered they could outsell the men. These are the heroes and heroines of the company. They have company
Chevys and expense accounts to take purchasing agents to

---

[1]A few years ago the line went, "Let me see if it's in the warehouse."

lunch. Every day they venture to the wars of the purchase order.

In the back section is the warehouse with its rows of racks of boxes. Sam has run this for years, but no one seems to know the names of the ever-revolving four ''kids'' who work for him. Three of the current four show up as a new set of nameless faces at every annual Christmas party.

Obviously, this unsavory description is only generally true. There are many exceptions where the quality of the selling and service exceeds that of the finest company direct sales force.

It must be remembered that distributors are independent companies, not agents such as manufacturer's representatives. They *own* your product once you sell it to them, and you have very little control over how they sell it, to whom, or at what price. On the other hand, they do take the *credit risks*.

Some effort must be made to define two additional loosely used and overlapping terms. *Dealers* perform a function similar to that of the distributor, but the term is more frequently used in relation to retail products. *Master distributor* suggests a two-tiered system where a large distributor covers a wide territory, selling to smaller, local distributors.

Value-Added Distributors

Also called value-added remarketers or dealers, these companies typically assemble your product into a system for resale to the customers. A rapidly emerging example is the computer dealer who will study a particular customer's need, then bundle together the computers (even several brands in order to match specific applications), the appropriate software, and perhaps a local area network to tie it all together. Despite their greater role in the marketing mix, most of what will be said later in this chapter about distributors in general, and need for your company's developing the desire for your product, directly with the end customer, equally applies.

A Comparison of Selfish Interests

Some marketing texts would have us believe that distributors are a natural companion organization to the manufacturer, with goals that are *complementary* to those of the manufacturer. This is not true, and the built-in conflict must be examined before the proper relationship can be understood.

Manufacturers, to maximize profitability, want the distributors to buy huge quantities of standard products, pay cash, and sell only to small accounts, leaving the larger ones as house accounts to be handled directly. Furthermore, they want any leads on "specials" or custom-engineered high-volume applications to be referred back to them and think that the distributor should then bow out and be grateful for the "thank you" received.

The distributors, on the other hand, to maximize profitability, want to buy from the manufacturers in hand-to-mouth quantities, pay after the customers pay them, and obtain nearly full markup on all custom or specially engineered products going to large accounts.

Despite these conflicting viewpoints, obviously, reason prevails and successful relationships are profitable to both parties; but it is important to acknowledge that these pressures are always present.

Finally, it must be said that successful distributors are that way because of an entrepreneurial spirit applied to *somebody's* products, so it might as well be yours. Now we will look at whether you should use distributors or not, and if so, how to make it a successful marriage for *your* products.

Do You Need Them?

The answer goes back to the critical question that underlies every marketing decision specifically, *what is the heart of the sales job to sell the particular product?* The sale of a custom-engineered, $500,000 chemical processing facility obviously does not have a role for a local store. At the other extreme, a manufacturer of commodities such as bolts and screws, resistors, or standard-size plastic sheets, must have many stores. In between, the decision may be more difficult. For example, how about a $1,500 electronic test instrument that is a standard design, or a specialty molding resin?

The analysis proceeds by first distinguishing between selling and distributing. *Selling* means getting your particular product specified and a purchase order written for it. *Distributing* means physically getting the product to the customer when it is needed. Distributors usually do only a part of the sales job, such as wrestling a specific purchase order from a competitor at the level of the purchasing agent. Only certain ones in certain industries are able to obtain your initial qualification as a vendor. So, first identify the specific, *entire* selling job, then see if distributors are a logical part of that strategy. If they are not, don't use them.

Too frequently the naive mistake is to set up distributors throughout a marketing territory, sell them the initial stocking quantities, bask in the enthusiasm of the distributor president and sales manager, and feel very complacent and glowing. This will last for as long as six weeks until the lack of reorders causes these same enthusiastic people suddenly to start complaining that the products are not moving. Obviously, the mistake was that selling to the *user* had not been taken into account.

Situations Requiring Distributors

Once the selling job to the user is identified and more than adequately provided for by other ingredients in the marketing strategy such as missionary selling or advertising, the following criteria may suggest the need for distributors.

- There is a widespread customer base needing small quantity deliveries, often frequently and promptly.
- The unit sale is small, their salespeople can handle the selling job and their complementary product lines provide a package of products large enough to justify the sales call.
- The products require no, or relatively little, *engineering* selling, but may require strong *purchasing* selling against direct competition.
- Local repackaging, simple fabrication, or even systems integration may be required. Examples range from plastic rod and sheet distributors who will cut to size to the computer firms mentioned earlier.
- The particular product or market traditionally uses them. (This does not mean the tradition cannot be broken, but one must be very aware of what effects a different strategy would produce.)
- The timing on the product growth curve is right. Products

that may characteristically and necessarily be sold through distributors may at first be best introduced by company direct sales people, selling to select customers. Later, as the product becomes known and accepted, it may be switched to distribution channels. Products of "medium" newness and a need for engineering sell may fall into this category.

Alternatives

After you have determined the need for distributors, several further alternatives must be considered.

Independent versus Company-owned Distribution

If your company already has sales offices in key locations, the alternative of renting some more space, hiring another person or so, and performing your own local distributing functions should be analyzed against that of using an independent distributor. With WATS lines and overnight delivery services, the role of the distributor has changed somewhat, and in many cases company stocks at fewer but key locations can satisfy customer needs and be more profitable to the manufacturer. The standard $1,500 instrument or specialty resins might be candidates for this type of supply.

Tangible factors that should be quantified in the analysis of which type of distribution to choose are:

- Difference in anticipated sales volume, if any.
- Difference in gross margin (and there will be a *big* one here favoring the manufacturer's doing the stocking).
- Increased selling costs versus reduced distributor support costs.
- Administrative costs of adding the function (rent, people, telephone, etc.).
- Effects on cash flow.

Two less tangible factors to consider are: much better control of your own inventories, and whether or not "different blood" could find some markets that would be otherwise overlooked.

The latter suggests a few words about the personal computer market where distributors and dealers have contributed, perhaps unwittingly, to pioneering market penetration. Here, I believe, the presence of so many outlets, all carrying directly competing lines, has significantly added to the tidal wave of mania for these gadgets. This market is so complex that a book-length case study could be written about it, but the deluge of magazines, newspaper articles, and user clubs are also segments of this snowball.

Local versus National Distributors

With a national distributor (or a few large regional ones), you gain the advantage of simplified administration (one contract does it all), maybe better customer service (if the product is not in one location they can ship from another), and the prestige of a nationally known name. The disadvantage is you get their bum branches along with the stars. Local distributors require much more work to choose and administrate, but you have the choice of the best in each area.

Heavy Coverage or Limited Distribution

Should you appoint only one distributor to a territory so it has little competition, or should you flood the area with every good distributor you can get? Here again the answer depends on the specific sales job required for the particular product. If you demand some selling effort at the purchasing agent level, then limit your distributors so they can have some incentive. If the product is a highly competitive commodity such as industrial lubricants or adhesives, then plug up all the distribution outlets you can and expect no active selling by the distributors. Rely instead upon your sales ''pull'' program, namely advertising or company salespeople, to create the demand.

How to Choose Them

The first step is to call on a sufficient sample of the purchasing agents of potential customers in the area and ask them to name the two or three distributors that would come to mind for your product. By asking that way, you do not place them in the position of showing favoritism. However, you may safely assume that the order of the names indicates their preferences. A more cost-effective way is to do the same thing by phone. Simply call the purchasing agents for your particular product, describe your firm and product, tell them you are setting up distribution and wonder who would be logical distributors for the product in their area.

Next, narrow the decision to not more than two. Phone the sales managers of noncompeting lines they handle, and ask them what their experience has been with that distributor. Four out of five times you will be amazed at the candor of the response. Ask specifically about the following:

- Field selling ability
- Promptness and accuracy in handling customer orders
- History of paying their bills
- General cooperativeness
- Feedback of their marketing data
- Overall rating on a 1–10 scale compared to the firm's other distributors

Obtain a Dun & Bradstreet or other credit rating. Use it only to see if they contain any "red flags".

Finally, pick the top contender (or two) and phone the president for a personal visit. Take special note of the following:

- How critically he or she evaluates you and your company. Too quick an acceptance is of concern.
- How enthusiastic the response is to your asking to meet the other people, particularly the salespeople. It is better still if they *offer* to have you talk with their people.
- How well organized the order-taking and warehouse procedures are.
- How much stock they seem to be carrying. When touring the warehouse, look at quantities of a few specific items as examples. Ask whoever is accompanying you if this is a typical stock of that product.
- The "gut feel" atmosphere of the place. Is it energy-charged, alive, fun, and enthusiastic; or drab, methodical, afraid, and defensive?

How to Live with Them (Joyfully)

The first step is to draw up a clear, concise, contract that is fair to both parties. As much as I dislike nurturing the current plague of societal rodents called lawyers, I suggest the contract be prepared by a capable attorney, experienced and knowledgeable in the fair trade laws.

The discussion of the distributor relationship should cover at least the following items. As many of these as legally possible should be defined in the contract.

- Sales staff and consequent effort to be expended
- Sales quotas
- General policy on pricing, referencing price lists for specifics
- Minimum inventory or reorder quantities
- Geographical territory
- Option to cancel if competitive products are taken on or other conflicts of interest arise
- Nonstandard items the distributor may stumble upon
- House accounts, if any, or any other conditions under which business may be taken directly by the manufacturer
- Reports or feedback to the manufacturer on markets or sales
- Training and technical support to the distributor by the manufacturer
- Responsibility for literature, samples, and other sales aids by both parties
- Terms of payment
- Handling of service or repairs
- Order cancellation
- Policy on returned products
- Product liability responsibility
- Special discounts to meet competitive pricing
- Support, if list prices are reduced
- Confidentiality
- Time period and termination conditions

The specific data or phrases to answer the above issues must be determined for each industry or marketplace because a "culture" has evolved around each. To discover what these are, first ask noncompeting manufacturers, then ask the potential distributors themselves what they want. While there may be some "asking for the moon," they will be surprisingly realistic. If you can reasonably grant their terms of contract, do so, but be firm and demanding in the results you expect. The respected manufacturer is fair, on the generous side, but tough on the expectation of excellent performance.

After the Contract

- Respond, respond. When they order their stock, ship it; when they ask questions, answer immediately.
- Train, retrain. Conduct seminars on the product. Repeat them as their people gain more experience, forget, and new people are hired.

A word of realism is necessary here. The results of training attempts will seldom meet your expectations because of your limited time in view of the number of distributor salespeople, a high turnover in some distributor sales forces, the "thinness" with which their attention is spread over a number of products, and their often less than adequate technical backgrounds. In an attempt to compensate for these factors, be sure you perform the following additional support functions exceedingly well.

- Provide outstanding literature, demonstration kits, technical manuals, or whatever sales aids are appropriate to the situation.
- Prepare these aids with the goal in mind that they would essentially stand on their own, even if mailed or presented to the customer by robot.
- Package the product to enhance the distributor's sell (display, shelf space, quantity increments, stacking, etc.), as long as the end customer is not compromised.
- Bring the distributor salesperson on engineering or specification sales calls. This is key to establishing a sense of partnership and results in the distributor salesperson being "hooked" on the account.
- Hold meetings at least quarterly where goals and results are reviewed, problems are listened to, causes of success are exchanged, and new product information is passed on. Start at 4:00 P.M., end at 6:30 P.M., and take everyone to dinner. Do *not* limit this to the president and salespeople. Frequently include Sam, the heretofore nameless faces, and the heretofore unmentioned office manager, Emily Sohrgum, who in reality runs the place.
- List the distributors in your literature and advertisements.
- Give pats on the back for work done well. Awards, including trips or gifts, can be valuable for encouraging performance toward predetermined goals.

Organizing to Handle Them

Who is responsible for this array of 36-hour-day activity? While some firms have separate, centrally headquartered distributor managers, I believe it should be the field manager of the territory in which the distributor is located; or if this job is large enough, someone who works for this person. It is also important that the field sales force be involved in the decision to use distributors and play the key role in selecting them.

When to Start Wondering If Everything Is Working

There are a number of danger signals to be sensitive to as life with your distributor moves along:

- There are too many requests for less than agreed-upon minimum stocking quantities.
- Small accounts are not being serviced. Only the big ones you could handle yourself attract their attention.
- Their sales growth is not paralleling that evidenced by other measures, such as direct sales, other territories, or noncompeting manufacturers.
- On your calls you hear customers too frequently mention a competitive distributor.
- There is a sudden surge of enthusiasm about your "great" product line, even though their sales are dropping and you have been secretly thinking about cancelling your contract with them.
- Payments slow down while sales reports show no increase (i.e., their cash flow bind is not due to your products booming).
- You spot furtive glances among their salespeople during your quarterly 4:00 P.M. meeting.
- James Olsen has stopped asking you to play golf.

In Summary

The decision regarding the use of distributors can be made only in the context of the decision on the entire appropriate marketing plan, which in turn comes from an analysis of "what does it specifically take to sell this product." If you find you need distributors, remember this most important factor. *In most cases, other parts of your marketing strategy such as direct selling or advertising must "pull" the product from the distributors' shelves.*

If independent distributors are utilized, a program of expectations and support must be continuously and zestfully carried on that will provide a return to you, the manufacturer, on the 15% to 50% gross margin they will carve off the top of the customer's price. This margin is above and beyond your direct promotional costs to create the "pull."

Your Plan

1. What type of product availability is required?
2. Is there a role for "value added"?
3. Are independent distributors the correct alternative to provide this?
4. If so, what specific functions will you expect from them?
5. How many distributors, where?
6. What qualifications?
7. What is your "selling to the customer" program that will "pull" the product through the distributors?
8. Is the overall program congruent with the distributors in terms of geography, types of customers, and product themes?

Product Support

I t is difficult to write about the subject of product support or service without sounding like "Mom and apple pie", but perhaps good support is of that nature. It means:

- The customers receive the product they expect (and, it is hoped, a little more) *when* they expect it.
- The product works even better than expected but when attention is needed (such as for installation, routine maintenance, or the *very rare* breakdown), it is provided with timeliness, enthusiasm, and from the bias that the customer is right.

Let us elaborate on each of these items.

Deliver the Product They Expect and More

The product ideally should be of a nature and packaged such that there is an element of pleasant surprise.

"That instruction manual was the clearest I've ever seen."

"I didn't know it included an extra filter."

"That dispenser package actually works."

When They Expect It

This means following three rules impeccably:

- Promise realistic deliveries.
- Meet delivery promises without fail.

- If there is the rare delay, inform the customer as soon as you know.

When selling through distributors, you as manufacturer have less control on these actions. However you can do some things:

- Continuously emphasize customer service to your distributors and let there be a "bite" in your message by eliminating those that do not serve the users of your products properly.
- Provide a toll-free telephone hotline number in all your literature so customers can call the factory. Have this manned at least over the full span of working hours, including time zone differences, and 24 hours if your product requires it. The person attending the hotline must be highly knowledgeable on all issues likely to arise and have the authority to promise proper corrective action.
- Be sure you and all your sales people are asking "How is the service we're providing?" when making calls on the user customers.

The Best Support Is a Good Product

As discussed in Chapter 7, the starting point of minimal service costs is in the design of the product. Design the reliability in, then manufacture it in. If a flaw does remain, then use the feedback from service calls to correct the problem immediately at the design or manufacturing stage.

Once this basic quality and appropriateness of the product is established, look for ways a little something extra can be added as a perk for the customer.

If the Customer Complains of a Problem

As your first priority, even before trying to figure out what went wrong, *get your customer's operation back running again!* This may mean air shipping a temporary replacement which you install immediately, before the defective unit is analyzed or repaired. Or it may mean bringing in a small supply of components to keep the assembly line running before a new purchase order can be written. Whatever it takes—*do it.*

Often you hear a salesperson say, in explaining a customer's complaint:

"It really wasn't our problem, it was the adjacent interfacing equipment."

"The idiots installed it wrong."

"They just wanted an excuse to send the shipment back because they over ordered."

While any or all of these can often be true, always start with the assumption that the customer does have a problem and you will fix it. (The rare company that tries to trick you into accepting a return because of excess inventory has two problems—one of inventory and another of ethics—and this will soon be evident to all.)

So, when you are notified of a problem, respond immediately. After getting things running again, investigate the problem thoroughly because you will likely find it to be different from what the customer initially described to you. In my own experience I cannot recall a single situation where the customer's description and analysis turned out to be complete or entirely correct. In many cases the analysis was quite erroneous. Investigate the problem with the customer's technical people if possible, so that they can feel ownership in the findings. You should *never* embarrass or humiliate a customer because the analysis given to you was wrong. Their participation in the study can corrrect their thinking with minimum embarrassment.

Remember, building a reputation for good service is a long and painstaking process but is easily and quickly destroyed with a few slips. In any industry the grapevine communications are speedy and thorough and the memories very long.

Your Plan

1. Are functionality and reliability designed into your product?
2. Are they manufactured in?
3. What training and service will or does your product require?
4. What is your plan to provide it?

CHAPTER
12

Literature

This chapter will tell you how to select the type of marketing communications literature needed, what it should include, and how to get it prepared.

A Cynical Perspective

Let us start with a story; one that may too frequenty be typical.

Rockhead Technology International, an old $20 million/year manufacturer of strain gauges, was getting ready to introduce a new line of ultrasensitive gauges; their first new product in five years. They were going "hi tech" according to the president. Bert Gollop, the new product manager who was formerly engineering manager on the project, called Bluken and Mohr Bluken, one of the better known marketing communication firms in the city. Malcolm Gastrone II, Senior Account Executive, responded and suggested luncheon at Au Dindon de la Farce, a new French restaurant.

The next Thursday, Bert met Malcolm, a very well dressed, slightly portly, pleasant fellow in his early 30s with a blow-dried haircut, who ordered a fine wine and instantly showed great interest in the product. He emphasized how his firm was dedicated to "working as partners" with growth firms like Rockhead and how personally he would like to be of service to Bert in launching this product. He pointed out how his staff of marketing strategists, media analysts, motivational assessors, focus group facilitators, market research specialists, and creative copy and layout personnel could work as partners with Bert to create "an effective marketing team." Bert had finished two glasses of a fine French wine and felt rather mellow. What Malcolm said sounded very good, particularly since Bert didn't feel too confident in all the aspects of marketing. He began to tell Malcolm, about all that had gone into developing the new product. By Malcolm's attentive expression and frequent nods, Bert felt he really understood the strenuous months of work that went into the product, and its technical capabilities.

By the end of the meal Bert suggested Malcolm do a product brochure. Malcolm responded immediately that this would be an excellent idea, and probably an eight-page, four-color design would be most appropriate for such an important product line—it would be very "hi tech" brochure. When they left, Malcolm said he would make a preliminary presentation in two weeks.

Bert was very impressed with the presentation. Malcolm brought Sheryl Somes-Jacoby, a very attractive blond woman whom Malcolm explained was their Director of Media Analysis and an MBA, as well as Jerold Smithers, who he explained was a market research analyst. Smithers was well dressed, slightly portly, and had blow-dried hair. Bert had Jim Dolkums, the vice president of marketing, sit in. The hour-long presentation included slides, viewgraphs, and a "mock-up" of the brochure which was unveiled page by page on its easel while a "strategic" description of each page was made. Jim whispered to Bert that maybe they didn't understand the product because "strain" seemed to be spelled "stain," and the prism-reflected laser beam on the cover had little to do with strain gauges, but Bert paid little attention since Jim had always been a cynic. Lunch followed at Au Dindon de la Farce and Bert was very happy.

To jump ahead in this tale, the brochure was printed at a final cost of $47,500. Bert's boss choked, his friends smirked, the salespeople said it was beautiful but didn't seem to describe the potential application in enough detail, and could they have some photocopied specification sheets please?

What was wrong? Obviously Bert did not know what he needed and the ad agency did what they do best—that is, sell their services.

I am obviously cynical about "corporate communications" firms, public relations, and advertising agencies, and everything I will say in this vein applies to all of them. I will take another swing and be more specific about ways in which many have a strong tendency to be parasitic nuisances when you do not take charge of your relationships with them and provide them with the information they need. First, they believe they are the entire marketing effort, not just a little piece of it as is usually the case with a technical product. Second, they presume they can write the brochure or ad without ever having personally presented the product to a customer and *seen* the emotional effects. Third, they have a character titled Account Executive who is paid twice as much as any of their creative people, yet who often is neither creative nor really understands your product or marketing strategy. This person performs, or delegates, a high-school-level coordination job between artists and printers, and stages outlandishly inappropriate "presentations" of the heartfelt work of an anonymous starving artist who is relegated to a tiny back windowless corner of their lavishly appointed offices. This "Account Executive" also buys you gourmet lunches, charges you for them at the end of the month, and finally tries to sell you more of the same.

I should state that in the consumer products area, where they are dealing with products with which they may have cleansed themselves that morning, account executives have done some remarkably creative marketing jobs. Their knowledge of and dexterity in the media infrastructure may serve them well in quickly positioning such a company and product prominently in the public's "valuing image." Furthermore, later in the chapter we will see how the relationship with a truly good and responsible agency *can* have very creative results.

Now that I feel much better, let us move on to discussing how to approach the question of the role of literature in your marketing mix, and how to go about preparing the material.

Where to Start

First and foremost, realize that as the *marketing wise* entrepreneur, who has looked customers in the eye time after time as you listened to their needs and explained your product, you and only you know best that special story that makes the customer's heart sing with glee, eyes dance with joy, and cheeks flush with pride. You know what is important and what is not. You know the particular words the customer uses. You have developed the strategy. This means that with whomever you work on literature, advertisements, or trade shows, you must assume a certain point of view. This point of view is two-pronged and goes as follows: First, *you as entrepreneur are the expert. You prepare the draft of the literature.* You are not intimidated by the agency's glitter and verbiage, which you know is meaningless. You have *final veto* on anything they do, and your "gut feeling" is probably the best judge. Second, you know that a truly creative writer or artist, who by definition must have deep insight into the human condition, can hone your rendition of "the story" into beautiful prose or stirring pictures—perhaps driving the story even closer to the archetypical levels in the customer's unconscious. You ask for their most creative effort, and for them to challenge your assumptions. Then you incorporate that which "feels right." The result can be greater than the sum of two separate efforts.

Now that bias is clear, let us move to more practical steps.

- Examine the strategy and determine the specific role the literature will play.
  - Does it have to do most of the selling job itself, as it might if the primary channel is through distributors, or is it an application bulletin to suggest more uses? The first requires a full story "salesperson stand-in" brochure; the application bulletin could be one page with a large photo of the product installation.
  - Is this a new product going out for selected customer trials, or a fully proven gadget needing an updated brochure? If the former, some neatly prepared photocopied technical data sheets marked "preliminary" would be most appropriate, whereas the latter may need a four-color brochure. If this is another in a series of similar products, such as a higher wattage resistor, a one-page information sheet to add to the others in the folder is appropriate. If it is a complex instrument and your company's only product, a six- or eight-page four-color brochure could be appropriate, because it must be a "salesperson" in your absence.

- Obtain all competitive literature to gain a perspective on what your potential customers are conditioned to seeing. Pick this up at trade shows, from distributors, or from friendly customers, or write directly to the manufacturer.
- Establish the basic literature concept in terms of the pieces needed and their basic message. The next paragraphs on the possible types of literature will help you determine the specific pieces you should use and their general form.

The "Menu"

Product Brochure

The brochure is fundamental to most marketing efforts and serves as an *igniter* and/or a *sustainer* of the customer's "valuing image" (discussed in Chapter 3). As an igniter, it may be used as a follow-up to an inquiry, sent as a direct mail piece, or given away at a conference. In one sense it is a poor but necessary substitute for a salesperson giving an actual product demonstration. The brochure can also sustain the valuing image when, after the salesperson leaves, the customer can sneak peeks at it to rejuvenate the feeling it originally induced, as well as show it to others.

The brochure must contain the following.

- A clear, preferably "in use" photo or photos of the product.
- "The story" that you have tested and honed until the greatest number of people react with a "twinkle and glow" suggesting positive unconscious material is being triggered. "The story" is not just a description and outline of benefits. Contrary to popular belief, benefits do not sell products—at least not until they *connect* with a feeling. Benefits are rationalizers. "The story" may also include a history of the product or inventor and some unique physical characteristics of the product.
- "Rationalization" aids such as benefits, comparisons to standard specifications or competition, and company background.
- Useful general technical data so it will be filed—not thrown out.
- Technical specifications, application, and interfacing information in summarized form. If complex, a separate manual should be prepared.

- Company address, phone, fax, WATS, etc., so further contact can be made easily.

The brochure can take several forms, but a good place to start is an $8\frac{1}{2}''$ × 11″, four-page version. (Actual number of pages will be determined by amount of data, your message and competition's brochures.) The cover should have a large, clear photo of the product in action, the generic and trade names of the product, and the company name. Inside, at the top left, is "the story" that makes the hearts sing. Following it are applications, benefits, and comparisons. On the back you might put specifications and company data.

The following are some situations and their respective literature requirements:

- *Product is new and only in test market.* In this case, prepare the above data (without the photo) in neatly typewritten form, and make photocopies. Mark the top "Preliminary Data Sheet." This then has the appearance of the "technical white paper" and in actuality is a tool to "test market" your forthcoming fancy brochure. Give it to the customers, ask them to scan it to see if it gives them the desired information. Note expressions, comments, and questions.
- *Product is an evolving family of separate products.* This could be the case with electrical components, paints, fasteners, tapes, and the like. Here you should structure the four-page brochure as a folder (perhaps with pockets), containing only data common to all of the products. The specialized information would then be put on single-sheet "Product Bulletins" that would be inserted in the folder in accordance with the customer's interests.

Company Capabilities Brochure

Generally this is not needed. A couple of paragraphs on the product brochure should do it. However, it *is* needed by a service company, and it may be useful as a summary for a company with multiple product lines.

Specification Sheets

This "plain white paper" document is written with format and topics paralleling the relevant government, industry, or customer specification—as applicable. It is a boring document, in fact a literary perversion, but a great aid in the rationalization process. The customers can simply transfer the data to their own specification format and be pleased that their day's work was made very easy.

Test Reports

Since credibility is crucial, test reports in traditional laboratory format also aid in rationalization. They have a scientific tone to them—particularly if prepared by an independent lab. Both they and the specification sheets are useful as excuses to make the second and third visits to the customer.

Application Sheets, Case Histories

This typically one-page "Here is still another way to use our product" or "Here is how Snurbultron Corp. used it" can be helpful in multiple application products where all the uses are not self-evident. If one of your customer's applications is shown, be *sure* to get permission and *clearly state this* on the sheet. It shows other customers you are responsible regarding proprietary data.

Technical Papers

Reprints of symposium papers are excellent handouts to potential customers and they can be quite information-filled and "scientific." They also can be furnished to editors for trade journal articles.

Price Lists

These should be separate sheets that are dated or date coded to facilitate changes.

Instruction Sheets and Operating Manuals

Typically included with the product, these should be very clearly written, with sharp, clear, and large photos or step-by-step drawings if necessary. Test them out on a number of customers, in addition to your not-so-bright neighbor, before finalizing.

How to Do the Literature

- All literature should reflect quality and good taste. Excessively expensive or glitzy pieces are as bad as poor quality, as they suggest lack of substance.

- For the brochure, *you* as entrepreneur, product manager, marketing manager, or whoever you are, should write it and make a rough layout as discussed earlier. Also ask two or three of your top, experienced salespeople to write their versions, including laying it out and suggesting the photos or drawings. (For specifications and other literature you may not need their input, however—just do it yourself.)
- Pick the best, edit, and rearrange into one or two alternative versions.
- Give these to an *outstanding* writer and an *outstanding* artist for the layout, making sure they work together, not sequentially. Tell them both that the draft represents marketing themes as perceived by the marketing people but they should criticize and suggest other ideas. I repeat, as product entrepreneur, *you* are the final judge and must be convinced. Do *not* defer to the artistic mystique if your marketing instincts tell you otherwise.

Where are the outstanding writers and artists? If you are a small company, use *free-lancers*, and avoid the costs of Malcolm Gastrone II. Find people by a relentless inquiry through friends, friends of friends, spouses, other employees, and local schools.

If you are a larger company, hire them. If you do want an agency, find out who did brochures for other firms that you found to be exceptionally well done.

How do you know if writers are outstanding? First, look at their work and reflect on your instinctive reaction. As you read it, do you feel:

- A sense of freshness, simplicity, crystal clarity, and humor? Hire the writer.
- It was written by the eighth-grade English teacher who ruined that year of your life? Let this one write your technical specifications, but never the sales brochure.
- It was written by a government agency. Don't bother to finish the sentence.

Next, call the people for whom your prospective writer has worked and ask them. Make sure that the writer was fully responsible for the work shown to you and was not merely collaborator or proof reader. Ask those employers to compare the writer on a one-to-ten scale with the most outstanding writer they have ever used, then find out who the top person was (and of course track him or her down for an interview also). Evaluating the lay-out artist (graphic designer) is the same process.

If You Use an Agency

Out of fairness to Malcolm Gastrone II and his kind, I must say that there are many talented, fairly priced (maybe) agencies who do excellent work for their clients. If you decide to use one, observe the following:

- When interviewing them, ask to meet their creative people. When talking with their writers or artists, ask about a tough challenge they have encountered and how they went about solving it. This will give you a feel for their creativity, zest, and overall capability. Ask about other work they have done. Watch their responses as you tell them about your products to determine if they can *really* understand your technology and marketplace.
- See what questions they ask you. Are they curious, and if so, can they ask the right questions to evoke the crucial information needed? For example, do they really try to understand the product? Do they ask in detail about your marketing plan and the role of the literature? Do they want to know the emotional reactions of the customers?
- If the decision narrows down to more than one agency, invite each to make a presentation on a specific requirement you will present to them. Ask that the writer and artist be at the presentation. Make it clear that this is to be a no-charge presentation.
- Obtain a very clear understanding of billing rates, and on any specific job, get a quotation.
- Avoid, or at least enter into with caution, monthly ''retainer'' relationships. This idling fee is usually more to the benefit of the agency than your company.
- Find out who their clients are, and even more importantly, about their *former* clients. When calling these clients, first check with the person at least one level above the person dealing directly with the agency; i.e., the vice president of marketing rather than the advertising director. This is because the person directly responsible may be particularly en-

joying the lunches. Of course, later get this person's reactions too. From former clients, find out why the agency is no longer used.

- After you have selected an agency, insist the writers and artists make some customer visits to get the emotional feel of the situation. Also insist that they in turn insist that you provide them with *your* drafts of "the story."

Your Plan

1. What role does literature play in your strategy, and what objectives must the literature meet?
2. What literature pieces are needed?
3. Draft a layout and write the copy for the key brochure.

13

Advertising and Publicity

I n this chapter you will learn what advertising and promotion are, what they can do, when to use them, and how to go about the task of promoting your product.

What Are They?

Advertising is page space for which you must pay. Publicity is the free stuff, the new product releases, articles, and mentions. Both are primarily "igniters" which one hopes will positively expand the *valuing image* in the customer's mind. Furthermore, both can aid in the *rationalization* process by reassuring the customer that the unconscious decision made earlier, which is now struggling to the surface, was for a product that is generally known and even part of the culture. (The solidity of the "brand name" or the reassurance of the parental archetype may be another way of thinking about this.)

Types of Ads

Product ads, by definition, deal primarily with the product itself and are a solicitation to the potential customer to get moving and buy some.

Image ads rise above anything as mundane as a specific product and attempt to posture the company in some exalted or self-congratulatory position as an industry guru, benefactor of mankind, font of creativity, or torch bearer of social responsibility. Recently, oil and cigarette firms have been using this type of ad to say they are nice. It would be interesting to trace the history of this concept, as I suspect it is one of the more creative self-serving products of the media industry. I cannot imagine a much easier sell than that of an opportunity for a president or chairman to pontificate in *Fortune* or *Business Week*.

Image advertising is sometimes done for specific purposes, such as recruiting or hyping undervalued stock prices. Generally, I believe that the best type of "image" ad is the *spirit-stirring product ad* about a *truly outstanding product*.

It Must Fit the Overall Strategy

The first and foremost rule is that there must be a very good reason to place ads to achieve sales. That is, you get more enhancement of the valuing image by advertising than through any other expenditure of your money. More specifically, you must want to "smoke out" additional customers who would be more costly to locate by other means.

Let us look at some examples of when and when not to use advertising.

Case I. Your company is an OEM supplier of private-labeled medical devices to the major firms supplying the intensive care field. You know all the potential customers (about 20) and are sellling successfully to 12 of them. Here any advertising or publicity would be unnecessary, a waste of money, and perhaps a public encouragement to competition.

Case II. You have introduced a new line of adhesives, have your distribution in place, know a number of industry applications, but do not know all the potential users. And besides, you suspect there are many other applications for the product. Here advertising and publicity must be a *predominant ingredient* in the marketing mix.

Case III. Your product or service involves a whole new way of doing things and you literally must *educate* your potential customers about the concept as well as tweak their valuing image. Examples might be local area networks, teleconferencing, and cellular phones. Here a series of ads describing what the world is like with these products is a vital part of the mix.

What advertising and publicity can do within an overall strategy might be summarized as follows:

- Generate inquiries and do so from potential customers you might otherwise never know.
- Make the personal sales job easier. Here the media message does some of the "valuing image" triggering that the salesperson otherwise would have to do.
- Bring about the buying decision—or nearly so. This may be the case when the product is relatively simple, little or no engineering is needed, and the product is sold through distributors. The advertising or publicity then triggers a high enough valuing image so the customer seeks out or is at least readily receptive to the distributor. Personal computer marketing is an example.

Considerations regarding the role of advertising/publicity in the strategy implementation are:

- *Timing.* It must be done at the time you want new inquiries. Do not do it during your field trial phase.
- *Coverage.* Ability to respond within the territory covered by the advertising is critical. If you are introducing the product on a region-by-region basis, you do not want to go immediately to national advertising.
- *Follow-up.* If you cannot respond promptly, first with literature, then with personal calls as needed, and finally with product in a timely way, the advertising will not only be useless, it will be quite harmful by creating a bad name for your firm.
- *Competition.* Have competitors created a level of advertising flack to the extent you have to match or exceed it to be seen as a factor in the field?

How to Do It

The comments I made in the preceding chapter on developing literature also apply here. My cynicism regarding the ilk of Malcolm Gastrone II pertains also to advertising and promotion—perhaps even more so. However, offsetting this is my even greater appreciation of the artistry of a copywriter or artist who can convert "the story" into a zinging message that resonates with the archetypes.

You, as a market-wise and customer-immersed entrepreneur, product manager, or marketing head, should *decide the strategy,* and *write* the copy. Then give it to a gifted writer and artist to tweak into pure poetry and vibrant art.

However, I will elaborate on a couple of additional points.

The *sociological structure* of the media industry should be examined for a moment. The agency people, space salespeople, and editors have a social circle and camaraderie around a common base. They tend to be educated, social people who find each other fun to talk with. There is much give and take between them, including lunching together and trading gossip, favors, and jobs. More important, however, and despite their self-illusionary grandeur, they share being on the outside looking in on the hard core of industry—the line managers making the marketing and sales decisions. Thus, while they enjoy talking to each other, they *prefer* to talk to you as the decision-making, innovating entrepreneur. It's a bit similar to members of a ball team fan club enjoying each other's company on the bleachers, but being far more excited about talking to a player.

Therefore, *cultivate your own relationship* with the editors of the trade publications relevant to your industry. Long before you want them to print anything for you, call them up on your trip to New York or Chicago (many are located in these two cities), take *them* to lunch, talk about your company, people, and products, and tell them to anticipate some articles. In addition to being hungry for something worthwhile to write about, they will see you as a potential advertiser, and will treat you very nicely.

Push publicity as far as you can before resorting to paying for ads. A new product release or article will generally draw as many leads as an ad, and is seen as a more credible presentation about your company than an ad. Agencies and space salespeople have a rap about the two supplementing one another, but do not believe it. One exception might be an industry survey article that does not give your company address and phone number. A nearby ad may help.

There is no need to use a flack mill to do your publicity since you should, and in fact must, write it anyway. As a guideline to writing it, study the formats used in the chosen magazines and simply do the same. Enclose a sharp 8″ × 10″ black and white glossy and phone your friend the editor to say it is on the way.

Ad Design

As stated earlier, you as the central figure on your product should be very clear about "the story" that warms the customers' heart about the product and exactly what you want a particular ad to achieve. Write the copy and make a sketch. Have two or three others who have seen the customers' eyes sparkle do the same. Then let your magicians take over.

Media Selection

In some industries the choice is obvious, as there are only one or two appropriate journals. In others, like electronics and computers, the array can be mind boggling. In this case, listen to the pitches by the magazine salespeople, study the Standard Rate and Data information, and listen to your agency (if you have one). However, in the final analysis, let what you learned from your data gathering (Chapter 4), regarding what the customers read, tilt your decision.

Your Plan

1. Do you need publicity/advertising to sell your product (i.e., what is its role in the strategy)?
2. When?
3. For what specific purposes?
4. Is it congruous with sales coverage, product timing, and other ingredients in the mix?
5. What is the theme or concept?
6. In what media?
7. Draft a sample of the ad.
8. Write the copy for a new product release.

CHAPTER
14

Trade Shows, Conventions, Technical Papers, and Seminars

T hese festivals, having become such an integral part of our culture that the economy of certain U.S. cities heavily relies upon them, cannot be overlooked as an ingredient to consider for the marketing strategy. Incidentally, I believe there are three reasons for their success:

- The archetypical need for annual rituals and the lack of them in other phases of our lives. Not every city has Mardi Gras. Furthermore, for many people the former magic of religious festivals has been lost and the annual round of Christmas parties has become a bit boring.
- The marketing zest of the trade association bureaucrats or show promoters and the attractiveness of their product—i.e., the satisfaction of companies' narcissistic need to be seen.
- The perks of a trip away from spouse and desk, much booze, conviviality with old friends, and maybe even the fantasy of the once-a-year secret romance.

These events have reached a critical mass in which companies feel compelled to exhibit or be "conspicuous by their absence" and employees feel "something is wrong" if their firm is not lavishly present. So let us examine this modern tribal ritual more closely. Do you really have to do it? And if you do, how?

Among others, there are three activities you can engage in at a trade show, singularly or in any combination.

- Simply attend
- Have an exhibit
  - On the main floor
  - On the "fringe," i.e., a suite
- Deliver a paper

Simply Attending

This is not simple if you do it well. "Well" means that in a span of two to four hours you survey the entire show, observing each booth and asking yourself:

- "What are the implications of this company's technology for us?"
- "What can I learn from their marketing presentation?"
- "Is it a competitor? If so, what are they doing? Do they have something new under the counter that they are flashing to special customers?"
- "Does anyone here impress me sufficiently to interview for our company?" If so, ask that person to give you a product pitch. If it's outstanding, introduce yourself and have a brief chat. Say something like, "You really know this stuff. Where did you study electronics?" You can learn a lot in a short time.
- "Is there anything about the booth presentation that triggers an idea for our display next year?" Idea: Immediately after the show, have all attendees "design" next year's booth in a short but intense brainstorming meeting.

Furthermore:

- Gather all remotely relevant literature.
- Listen to the conversations going on around you.

When you complete your tour, go to the registration counter and buy reprints of the technical papers. This avoids the unendurable boredom of listening to them, since you most likely read much better than they talk (or read aloud). The above is the minimal tour. There are times to stay around a couple of days and "soak" in the atmosphere of it all, meeting people, actually listening to the presentations of papers, participating in the question and answer follow-up, noting who asks certain questions, and going to the various company "open house" alcoholic gatherings. Good reasons to stay, outside of basking in company-paid rest and recreation, could be:

- This is a new market for your company and you are trying to learn the "culture."
- You are new to the job and need to get a "feel" for the people and attitudes.
- You are trying to meet someone specific whom you cannot reach otherwise. (Call that person's office and ask where he or she is staying, or ask for the staffing schedule at the company's booth.)

Remember that everyone is there in a mood to talk business. If you have shyness problems, this is the time and place for testing non-shy behavior. Do not be held back by normal social etiquette such as not interrupting ongoing conversations or not barging into a circle where you may think the people all know each other. The group in front of you did not know each other five minutes ago, and each got into it by joining in just as you are about to do.

Who Should Attend

If you are a new company and the show is nearby, everyone should spend half a day.

If you are old and jaded, or your company is, and everyone has attended every year, think twice. However, shows are still excellent market education opportunities for:

- New employees who need to get a "feel" for the industry.
- Longer-term employees who have forgotten what the customer is like.
- Employees from engineering, production, and administration who need a closer picture of the marketplace.
- People writing and designing your sales literature and advertisements. They should obtain competitive literature and listen to the terminology, spirit, and attitudes in which the products are discussed.

Having an Exhibit

An exhibit floor is a peculiar thing. Hundreds, and perhaps thousands, of your actual or potential customers pass in front of your booth, numb, and with eyes glazed from the combined effects of sensory overload and hangovers. Your people, suffering from the same numbness, feign a pose of vulture-like readiness to leap at the right name tag, or at least to respond with strained alacrity to someone momentarily stopping. Should you participate in this gathering of zombies?

What You Can Achieve with an Exhibit

- *Identify and start relationships with additional prospects.*
  - *From existing accounts.* For example, you may have had trouble reaching your contact's boss or an engineer in a certain department, but he walks by your booth—and you leap.
  - *New accounts.* This can be particularly important when you are trying to reach a new market. The various directories of companies in a certain field are likely to miss some key possibilities, who may be attending. Particularly convenient and economic may be the opportunity to make contact with visiting foreigners.
- *Further established relationships.* While time pressure prevents very much from being done, a few words with someone who has your product under test may save the next planned sales call.
- *Expose new products for feedback prior to final release.* This requires some cautions. First, it is a blatant exposure to competition. Second, it should be clear to everyone seeing it that the product is not yet available, so there are no unfulfilled anticipations. However, it is a way to obtain feedback fast.
- *Enhance company image.* An appropriately done booth gives everyone who sees it a tangible impression of your company, people, and products, and shows that you are real and a solid factor in the industry.
- *Trigger further publicity.* Trade publication editors wander the aisles of these technical flea markets looking for something that is even slightly new and interesting. If it is part of your marketing mix at this time, have an article written in news

release form ready for them. Treat them well—mainly by explaining at a technical level they can *really* understand how your product works and why it is different.

- *Impress the financial community.* Increasingly, venture capitalists, investment bankers, and bank loan officers are wandering around these hype-tech bazaars, looking for what is new and promising. If you need financing and they contact you, it is a much better starting point than your calling them.
- *Expose your non-salespeople to the customer.* This can be quite beneficial to both attitude and actual performance, particularly with development and production people.

What Are the Negatives?

- *Costs.* Well beyond the direct booth, hotel, travel, and outrageous entertainment costs are the alternate opportunity costs. What other things could your people be doing in the same time?
- *Competitive exposure.* You can be sure your competitors will learn as much about you as you about them.
- *Creating something you are not ready to handle.* You *must* be ready to screen the leads immediately, send literature, and call on the key prospects. If you are not set up to do so, it is worse than not showing at all.

When Should You Exhibit?

The answer should be obvious by now. We must ask the question we always go back to—what is the essence of the job of selling the product to the customer? If the job to be done requires the things an exhibit can do, then it is more likely to be an appropriate part of your marketing plan. The following are some situations where exhibits fit.

- You are introducing a new product, it is in production so deliveries can be made, and you have sales coverage in the territory the trade show would draw from. However you do not know a sufficient number of the potential customers.
- You are a new company, or entering a new market, and need both to be known and to know others—including customers, competitors, and vendors—and of course you are prepared to respond to inquiries.

- You are in an industry where the shows inherently play a big role, even to the extent of order-taking at the show.

Incidentally, holding a sales meeting or retraining program for your sales people just before the show is often economical and effective.

How to Prepare the Exhbit

- Apply for floor space early to get a high-traffic location; i.e., a corner, main aisle, or proximity to entrance.
- Choose a size appropriate to your company and the nature of your show. Too large and lavish a booth makes people wonder. For a small, growing company, the "second size up" is often right.
- Register early enough so you can get an articulate product description in the show directory.
- Design the booth. As entrepreneur of the product, who has seen the look in the customers' eyes and heard their specific words about your product, *you* "design" the booth before giving it to a booth designer, according to the following guidelines.
- Display the company name and generic name of the product prominently. If your company is not known, emphasize the generic product name. If you are a DuPont or GE, the company name is more of a stopper. *Never* make most prominent the razzmatazz trade name you are so proud of, "XZESTAR P 2000i3," since unfortunately it will mean nothing to anyone (their minds are trashed enough already) except you.
- If the product is small, e.g., an electronic component, use large color photos on the backdrop with a showcase of actual samples in front. In some cases a video of the product in use can be effective.
- If the product cannot be given as samples, have some openly displayed so they can be *touched*. You may want to chain them down, but the very act of touching them conveys a meaning and depth of impression to the customer that merely viewing cannot.
- Provide a demonstration of your product if it lends itself to that in any way. The ideal is where the attendees do the demo, quickly and without malfunction, then can take their sample, identified by your company name, with them. For

example, a fastener product would lend itself to this type of demonstration.

- Write the few precisely stated product description and benefit lines you may want displayed.

Now, turn your design over to a talented booth designer for the touch of magic and detail of color, construction, and form.

Select the designer using the methods I suggested for finding a good brochure writer. Also, if you attended an earlier trade show, you should have asked the companies with particularly effective booths who did them.

How to Run the Booth

- Use the product, if at all possible, as the people-grabber. Companies have been able to attract hordes with magicians and stand-up comics, but I doubt if many of the enthralled knew what the company made.
- Attractive booth attendants will increase the number of people stopping. But the days of sexist costuming are over, and *all* booth workers must be fully *technically competent* on all products and able to present a sense of quality to the customers. Incidentally, gimmicks like Texas hats or plaid vests usually make the attendants look like jerks and, worse, act like jerks as they attempt to play out the roles suggested by their embarrassing costumes.
- Treat *all* passersby with courtesy, including competitors (at least you want their respect, and you may want to hire one of them later), sample grabbers, jerks, pigs, people with upside-down name tags, and punks. You simply never know how it will ultimately affect you. Of course, get as many names, addresses, and job functions as possible. Most shows now use cards to make this easy.
- Alert your booth attendants to key people to whom you want special attention given.
- Once the show is over, respond rapidly. Screen the leads and categorize them by levels of importance; e.g., immediate personal call, routine call, literature only. Keep a file of them. Send all, except competitors, a cover letter and appropriate literature immediately. Note the ones requiring personal follow-up, and *see that it is done promptly.*

Evaluating Results

This is difficult, and there is little that can be objectively done. However, the following steps may lend some perspective:

- Count the important leads and relate them to show cost. Compare this to what could have been done by the same people if the show had not happened and they had spent time in exploratory calls.
- Reconsider this six months later and see what these leads turned into.
- Mull over the other things that happened. A scientist with a new but related technology stopped by. Three people who look good want to work for you. The representative of a venture capital firm showed some interest.
- Realize that next year you still will not be sure it's worth it.

Hospitality Suites

The desirability of these gatherings resists generalization since the practices within each indusry vary widely. Generally you should start with the bias that they are a costly way to provide a drinking spree for people you already know and freeloaders whom you never will, or want to, know. However, in some industries they are part of the expected activities, particularly if you are a large company in the field. Furthermore, a suite can be a good place to have relaxed talks with the top management of your customers or other key individuals. In such cases, have your products on display, invite selectively, and try to sustain your vitality and courage.

Delivering a Paper

Technical papers can be an effective ingredient in the marketing plan. We will examine how and under what circumstances, but first let us look at the typical motivations of a person presenting a paper.

- *Job hunting.* This can be for exposure to evoke immediate offers or for "resumé building."

- *Alternate recognition.* The person feels insufficiently recognized within the home company and seeks outside attention.
- *A combination of above.* Unsuccessful job hunting but satisfying alternate recognition results in the Professional Paper Presenter, or P^3—to use that modern grammatical obscenity, the exponential acronym. The P^3's life is dedicated to preparing the next paper, having given up, after the fourth one, any hope of its leading to the new job. However, after the third paper came election to the "prestigious" post of Membership Chairman of the Association. Incidentally, the boss is typically satisfied with this arrangement since the papers do help promote the company. Old Joe always knows what is going on in the industry, and best of all has not asked for a raise for over two years.
- *Sales promotion.* This is the most common motivation, where someone such as the marketing manager simply dictates that a blatant pitch, disguised as a "technical paper," be written on a new or retread product.

What a Paper Can Do

- Stimulate direct product inquiries.
- Become an excellent piece of sales literature, for either direct mail or handout, which is more credible than a sales brochure.
- Serve as the basis of a trade publication article.
- Build company prestige. A particularly good way is to have a prestigious customer deliver the paper.

Do Present a Paper

- If it fits the needs of the specific marketing job to be done.
- To stimulate new leads.
- To enhance the image of the firm.
- To help establish credibility of a new technology.
- If you really have something to say.

Do Not Present a Paper

- If the product strategy is to target sales to accounts with direct selling and minimize stimulation of competition. (The

competition will know, but may place lower priority on responding if you do not make a public show of strength.)
- If you are not set up to respond to interest generated, either
from sales, service, or product availability.
- If the time required for preparation can be better spent elsewhere.
- If you are a lousy speaker.

If by reviewing the criteria for presenting a paper you determine that it is a key ingredient in support of the basic marketing
job to be done, then the following guide may be helpful.

How Not To Write A Paper

First I will describe the outline and "formula" for the majority of
papers presented at almost any convention you may attend. To
do so accurately, I must resort to presenting the following satirical
structure.

TITLE

Summary
  History
  "Solid state herkygrams were first introduced in 1982.
Since that time many improvements have resulted in . . ."
(Start by softening up the audience by extending a few posi-
tive but irrelevant tidbits as to what others have done.
Then move to a gradual degradation of the competition by
showing how they evolved to a very fine state in several
inappropriate areas, while the real needs have not been met.
These real needs, of course, coincide with the features your
yet-to-be revealed product offers.)
  Present State of the Art
  "A survey of requirements versus existing components
showed that . . . (Now you start some heavy flailing. Support it with charts showing "survey data" and lab test results. Of course the survey also shows the needs to be the
features of your about-to-be-revealed product.)
  Recent Developments
  "Recent developments have resulted in a new generation
of herkygrams that withstand 300°C in the normal under-
water environments . . . (This is the *unveiling*. In the interests of noncommercialism and humbleness you normally

do not mention your company by name, but of course your label is prominently displayed on the product.)

Test Data

(Here charts are shown with the test data of your "recent development" pitted against the pitiful competition on those "features" the "industry needed?" This is the clincher, the final wipeout of competition.)

Conclusions and Future Implications

"Herkygrams were examined in view of current environmental demands and found to be inadequate in several areas. To meet these new, high-performance requirements, a new generation of herkygrams has been developed. It is anticipated that industry standards will be re-evaluated in light of these developments."

The preceding "guidelines" were given for a product. If you should be selling a service or management consulting concept, the same steps apply, but conceptual charts must be added. Here the goal is to present the unquantifiable mishmash of real management as a quantifiable "management tool." This is done using a four-quadrant chart.

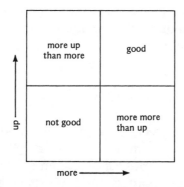

Actually this inane chart is a composite taken from recent issues of the leading management publications.

Now that the paper is written, the question is how and by whom should it be presented? At present, most speakers fall into one of the following categories.

- *The "Next Slide Please" Mutterer.* The opening greeting is a grunted "First slide please". Then a series of slides follows, accompanied by rumbling sounds that turn out to be the reading of the bullet statement on each slide concluded by "next slide please." (In one reported instance the rumbling stopped twice in one speech when the engineer speaker leaned over to pull up his unmatched white socks.)

- *The Reader.* This too is a slide show, except here the presenter reads the full script in a monotone punctuated by the syncopated clicking of the slide projector.
- *The P³ (Professional Paper Presenter).* This is similar to "the reader" except the material flows by heart, and jokes three decades old are programmed into the first half. (The first two get an empathetic but embarrassed laugh from the front row.

Incidentally, the use of viewgraphs and slides may have done more to curb good oratory than any other invention. Think of what it would have been like if Lincoln had used a viewgraph in delivering the Gettysburg Address.

All Cynicism Aside

The key to a successful paper should now be obvious. A paper with the preceding format but of integrity, objectivity, and technical substance, presented with naturalness, clarity, spontaneity, and relevant humor, is like an oasis in a desert, and a company making such a presentation can gain instant esteem from the typically 50 to 400 attendees.

Sponsoring Company Seminars

These can be a very effective means of extending contacts in one or several neighboring companies. They can be used to introduce a product or to extend applications of an existing one. They provide an opportunity to contact and invite bosses without subordinates feeling you are going around them. Large or complex equipment that cannot normally be carried to a customer's office can be set up and demonstrated.

A typical format is as follows:

- Rent space at a convenient and respected hotel.
- Work very hard on inviting the right people, including calling the preceding day to remind them.
- Start the seminar as early as possible after working hours; i.e., 5:30 P.M.

- Serve refreshments for only as long as it takes for each person to get one drink.
- Have products on display and literature at each seat.
- Give an exciting 30- to 45-minute presentation full of "real meat"i.e., containing technical and applications data. Perhaps have the inventor or R&D specialist give part of the presentation. Allow 15 to 20 minutes for questions.
- Be sure enough company representatives are there to engage in subsequent conversations (one company person for every five to eight customer people).
- Break the formal meeting for hors d'oeuvres (delicious ones) or dinner (also delicous—Chapter 8 tells you why) and an open bar. Company people now should intensely mingle. Continue this as long as your guests stay.
- *Never, never* have a long cocktail hour, dinner, and *then* the presentation—which is often the format. During dinner there is nothing to talk about except children, golf, and general gossip, and after dinner you have nothing but sleepy "drunks" dozing through your presentation.
- Within three days call every attendee, thank them for attending, and ask if they would like any further information. If people from several or even competing companies were present, there might have been some reluctance to ask certain questions.

Your Plan

1. Are conventions or seminars necessary to promote your product (i.e., do they play a role in the strategy)?
2. When?
3. For what specific purpose?
4. Are they congruous with sales coverage, product timing?
5. Which shows, where, how large a booth?
6. Sketch the booth.
7. What role could technical papers play?
8. What do you have worthwhile to present?

PART
THREE

Making It All Work

Organization
and Motivation

Who You Hire

Always seek the "best." You must staff the *top* of your organization with the best because less talented people generally cannot hire someone better than they are. For example, the caliber of your sales manager is the ceiling on the caliber of all subsequent salespeople. Backing up one step, the overall caliber of the president determined the caliber of the sales manager in the first place. The only qualification to this is that people of wisdom, good judgment, and a sense of personal security can hire and manage people more technically qualified than they are. This assumes that they facilitate and do not hamper the growth of these people.

Furthermore, you should hire overqualified people and then structure the environment so they can grow the jobs to their capacities.

Where You Find Them

If your company is large enough to have the luxury of training inexperienced people, the obvious source is the top students from the top schools. For experienced people, look for those who have had previous employment with the companies who select those students just mentioned. Hewlett-Packard, IBM, DuPont, and

Procter and Gamble are examples of such companies. Generally go for those who are not looking for a new job, since they obviously know how to function well. The exception is that some very good people in large companies get an entrepreneurial itch after a few years (maybe three to five—after that they may be imprinted with bureaucracy) and are out looking. If they have outstanding track records it is probably a very good sign.

Regarding the ethics of hiring people away from seemingly happy jobs, I must state my attitude, which may be a bit radical. I feel that as long as the new job is described honestly and entirely, it is acceptable to "raid" someone, and in turn I would expect and accept such a "raid" on my people. In fact, I would go one step further and state that if knew of a better outside opportunity for my most valuable employee I would tell that employee about it. My reason for this attitude is twofold: First, I believe helping a person find a more fulfilling life is a value higher than selfish corporate interests; and second, if you cannot provide sufficient stimulation and rewards to enable your employees to withstand such onslaughts then you are not properly utilizing them and in turn your company is suffering.

You should always be collecting names for a "people inventory." Ask your friends who were the top people in their classes, or in prior work situations, and what are they doing now. Ask friendly customers who the best salespeople calling on them are. If you are interviewing, ask the interviewees to rate themselves against the best peer they know. Then casually ask for the name of that peer. Your own employees are one of the best sources. In fact, a substantial bonus if a recommended person is hired can be a good incentive. Since a head hunter's fee is at least one third of a year's salary, you can afford a few bucks. Finally, trade shows and conferences are good places to get first impressions of many people.

From all these sources, list those that seem to be the best of the best and plan to interview them on your next trip to their territory. Call and explain that you have a policy of interviewing before the actual opportunity arises, and you would like to acquaint them with your firm and get to know them for possible future consideration. They will be flattered, and even more important they will not have to face the acceptance/rejection confrontation one does when interviewing for an immediate opening. In addition to practicing this "people banking" yourself, expect your other key people to do so. The "bounty" mentioned above may help them keep it in mind.

The use of a reputable head hunter who is a specialist in your industry is fine if these other measures do not produce the people you need. In fact, the cost of finding and hiring good people, as outrageous as it seems, is the *very best investment you can make*—spare nothing. One correct decision made by a qualified employee can repay the search costs many times over.

A final caution. When hiring from competitors, do *not* hire for the person's competitive knowledge. It is basically unethical, and furthermore is an open invitation for a lawsuit. If you wish to hire such people for their basic capabilities, do so under the guidance of good legal counsel.

How to Evaluate Them

The final criteria are that you and several of your people-sensitive associates feel *unqualified enthusiasm* for hiring this person and that careful reference checks—with bosses, peers, and subordinates (especially those with whom there may have been disagreements)—reveal respect and admiration for the person. This does not mean the candidate cannot be human and have weaknesses, but the enthusiasm must prevail after these frailties are understood. One test is how you feel at the end of the interview. If you want to continue to chat and even have the person participate with you in your next task you feel this enthusiasm. If you think, "What a competent person. I'm sure he'll do a good job. Oops, where are my papers for the next meeting?" then the enthusiasm is lacking and you probably should not hire the individual.

There are many books on interviewing, so I will make only a few specific comments on this subject.

The majority of your questions should be open-ended, allowing the greatest freedom to answer. For example, "Tell me about your previous job" is potentially more eliciting than "What were your responsibiltiies in your previous job?" It is likely to open up new trails. If your instincts tell you there is something to be learned there, pursue it.

Watch carefully for signs of tensions and gently pursue those subjects that you perceive relate to the tension. You might even acknowledge it by saying, "That event seems to have left you with conflicting feelings.'' The candidates' evaluations of their weaker areas can be quite revealing and show how self-aware and honest they are. It also is a clue to whether they can even discuss the issue of their personal work habits. The oft-heard answer "My main weakness is that I'm a workaholic" is of course a diversion, or evidence that the person is out of self control, and should be pursued further.

One way of asking about weakness I have found effective is, "If I could hear all the candid opinions your prior work associates have about you, what would they be?" or, "In your previous reviews, what are both the positive and negative items brought up?"

Much can be learned about a person's style, "world view," and emotional makeup by knowing about their outside-of-work activities, family, and even record in early schooling. For example, evidence of leadership strength can be looked for very early in a candidate's life, such as school committee organizing, sports team leadership, and attitudes of peers and subordinates in earlier work situations. You should thoroughly check prior work situations. Certain personality types, including some with severe character disorders, can be very charming, having developed the skills of adapting and resonating with everyone they meet. Without a clear core personality and consequent sense of self, without the inhibition of shyness or the ethical restraints of a functioning superego, they are the "con artists" who drift from sales job to sales job. They may be quite successful in the one-time sales situation but for prolonged sales relationships they are of course a disaster.

Checking references is getting more difficult as the mass paranoia regarding law suits results in more companies declaring policies of confirming only the employment dates of former employees. I know of no easy way around this except to try anyway. If you find that a company has such a policy, get the candidate's specific approval on calling a reference and phone that person at home—stating that so-and-so (your candidate) suggested you call. The conversation should be more relaxed in this setting. If the reference recites the company policy, you might try a response like, "I'm inclined to interpret this to mean there may be some negative aspects that are quite delicate to discuss?" Now listen carefully to the emotional tone of the response. If it is an instant, "Oh, no. The person was great. It's just a new policy the company has that we cannot discuss such matters," then everything is probably satisfactory. If there is a long pause or some comment like, "I cannot respond to that," then be a bit suspicious.

You might try having the candidate write a letter to the potential reference, with a copy to you, giving permission to speak candidly to you.

Another approach is to find someone who has left the company (your candidate may be able to help) and hence is not feeling the restrictions of the policy. Still another is to contact someone you or an acquaintance knows as a friend in the company. As an "insider," he or she can probably find out your candidate's reputation there.

I will offer a few tips on questioning references:

- The issues you will want to ask about include overall performance on the prior job, intelligence and capacity for growth, selling style and results, people-managing skills or potential, ability to get things done within the organization, relationships with others, technical depth, judgment, creativity, and integrity. Another approach is to ask about the person's strongest areas and weaker ones.
- As much as possible ask each question with a yardstick attached. For example: "On a one-to-ten scale, where would you rate her judgment?" "Of all your salespeople, where in an array would you place him?" "If you think back over her career, can you recall one instance where you had a question regarding integrity?"

  The general question brings a general answer. Example: "Was he good at sales?" Answer, "Yes."
- Preface your question about weakness in a way that assures an answer. Example: "She sounds outstanding. Of course we all have things we are better at than others, and if you were to indicate the two or three areas on the opposite end of her spectrum, what would they be?" In contrast, if you were to ask, "What are her weaknesses?" the answer might be a safe, "None I really know of.

The use of psychological testing may be a question in your mind by now. My own opinion, in spite of my academic work in psychology, is mixed and uncertain. I have some unresolved ethical questions about *requiring* a person to go through mechanistic testing to be eligible for consideration. I have doubts about the value of any mechanistic, "computer scored" testing service. On the other hand, a sensible and sensitive psychologist can effectively use testing to more quickly identify issues that may need discussion. Testing may raise a red flag on deep-rooted disturbances, and finally "type" testing such as Myers Briggs may only give a rough clue to a person's "style" of functioning. For example, a very high rating on "sensation–thinking" should assure you that this person would be looking at the numbers and justifying plans with beautifully concocted logic. However, present fair hiring practices legislation requires that any testing be demonstrably relevant to the job requirements. This in turn probably means that the test was validated on present employees performing the job. The marketing and sales jobs under discussion here are complex and sophisticated, requiring a person with complex and sophisticated traits. In view of these factors, I think finding or devising a meaningful and legal test is a task not worthy of the effort.

Where a large sales force is already in place and in turn a large number of people are screened for a relatively simple selling job, the likelihood that a legal and useful screening test can be devised is greater.

In concluding this evaluation section I must state one rule. Hiring someone can be compared to contemplating marriage. If you have to "decide," don't do it.

How You Recruit Them

The key here is involvement, an emotional connection, a feeling on the part of the candidates that this organization is where they belong and the people are ones they will feel proud to consider their friends and associates. Certainly salary, bonus, opportunities, and even benefits get talked about and even have an element of importance, but they are not the arena in which the decision is made any more than cost effectiveness comparisons are the basis of our customer's decisions. How do you bring about this involvement? The answer is "many ways," including:

- Have your candidates bring their spouses or significant others, and have these people also tour the company, meet a number of key people, and even be present at several of the interviews.

- Have the candidates meet key top management, peers, and subordinates in addition to those encountered in the multiple interviews.
- To the extent proprietary discussions allow, have candidates sit in on a meeting or two, or at least a four-minute decision-making spasm in the hall with an associate, in which your candidate may even be asked for an opinion.
- Have a social gathering such as a dinner or cocktail party where spouses and significant others of those that will be working associates can get to know each other.
- Be "authentic." If this turns off the candidate, then the association should not be anyway.

How You Train Them

Very well! This means weeks and maybe months in the factory and with experienced salespeople as well as in more structured classlike settings for product knowledge training. After formal product training, it is most helpful if new people can do a stint in supervised product design and then customer service jobs. Learning by wrestling with and solving real-life problems teaches to a depth that "learning about" never can.

People who are in training for a sales job will not be appreciated by the customer. They have to "hit the ground running."

Regarding "sales" training I would recommend the following:

- The sales manager or a good trainer to teach the material discussed in Chapter 8, using experiences and role playing. The latter, while sometimes seeming stilted and awkward at first, can readily become an exciting learning experience.
- A course or seminar in listening, plus another in reading body language.
- Perhaps a course in situational leadership to broaden the span of personalities and situations effectively dealt with.
- Continual field training in which it is understood that when the sales manager travels with the trainee a "post-mortem" (both ways) is a useful, skill-improving experience and not an opportunity for mutual personal degradation.

Two "far out" ideas I have had for some time, but not used, are to train for developing a sense of self and balance using the Japanese martial art "Akido," and to improve listening abilities by using a skilled clinical psychologist as instructor.

By now you must realize my negative bias regarding many of the glitzy, packaged sales training programs which can push a quite reasonable but slightly insecure person over the border into being a hyped, programmed automouth.

How to Organize Them

Under a vice president of marketing (which by definition includes sales—right?), who in a start-up may do the entire marketing and selling job, the following people may be appropriate.

Sales Manager

Depending upon the size of the company, this individual could supervise international, national, or regional sales. The job is first and foremost that of leader and coach. The person filling it must possess characteristics such that the field salespeople trust him or her to represent their interests to higher management, to help them with difficult situations, to pave paths to higher opportunities, and to see that their achievements are recognized personally and financially.

The sales manager needs a combination of personal leadership, outstanding selling, teaching/coaching, and organizing skills. The latter are needed to assist the salespeople in territory planning, priorities, and time management. On balance, the personal leadership area is probably most important.

The sales manager must have outstanding selling ability to serve as a role model, to teach, and actually to perform in the rare situation where a salesperson needs "bailing out" of a customer situation that went askew. With proper training and coaching, this should not happen—but when it does, it may simiply be due to personality differences between the salesperson and the customer.

Field Salespeople

These people are "the company" to your customers and should not be representatives, agents, or go-between people. Thus the salesperson must be a personal technical resource to the customer, someone who can solve problems, teach, analyze situations, make decisions, and answer questions. Thus, you should spare nothing to get the most competent people possible. First and fundamentally they must have the technical education to respond to new situations with depth. This means that their understanding comes from a *knowledge of science*, not from the facts and figures on brochure sheets. For selling a technical product this probably means a science or engineering education.

With the above as a base, they must be *doers*, not satisfied until the end result is achieved. I have too frequently observed failures that result when technical salespeople become so intrigued with the customer's technical problems that "asking for the order" never occurs to them—they like the "process" more than the results.

Of course, salespeople must have interpersonal skills and engaging personalities based upon a *true interest* in others. Social skills of feigned interest and colorful joke telling do not carry very far in sales requiring long-term relationships.

Finally, some of those hired should show evidence of the characteristics mentioned above for sales manager and product manager so they can later advance to these jobs. For those whose interest or balance of skills makes them better suited to staying in sales, the company should provide an alternate advancement path to "Senior Sales person" or something of the sort, carrying with it pay and prestige comparable to positions in the management path. Each salesperson should be assigned a clear-cut territory defined by geography and/or customer type.

Product Manager

The role of this person in a company is best described by an analogy to an entrepreneurial situation. Imagine an entrepreneur who has a product and some capital, but no physical resources under direct control to exploit the product. What happens? A contract with a manufacturing firm to produce it at a certain price, to agreed-upon specifications, and on a certain schedule is executed, followed by the establishment of a team of manufacturer's reps to sell the product. An arrangement is made with a product development laboratory to design improved and new products. The entrepreneur then acts as a juggler, keeping all of this in motion, coordinated, growing, and profitable. It involves spending much time with customers and salespeople to develop an ongoing understanding of the market, analyzing the data, creating the marketing plan, and then implementing it. The product management job in a larger company should be just this—except that the production facility, "reps" and product development lab are of course within the company, and the product manager is competing with other product managers for corporate time and these resources. Priorities for the particular product line, however, including production scheduling, are the product manager's responsibility. The characteristics needed include average or better selling ability, but more important a sensitivity, perception, and skill in articulating the selling situation so that the strategy is defined, "the story" is properly written for the brochure, and the field salespeople are properly trained. The product manager needs good judgment, organizing and coordinating skill, and the interpersonal skills that facilitate getting people to do things even though they are not in the same organization. Their quantitative performance measurements should be on sales growth and gross margin contribution.

Market Manager

This is exactly the same job as that of product manager, and requires the same skills except that it deals with a number of products within a single market or market segment, whereas a product manager deals with one or a single family of products to all markets. Again, this position should carry with it priority-setting authority.

Obviously, if your company has one product to one market you have a lot of freedom in labeling the person in this job.

How to Motivate Marketing People

For anyone in the marketing and sales management role the following are key items to keep in mind. Motivation comes primarily from recognition, appreciation, and participation in decision making, which in fact is actually a high form of recognition. Praise your people immediately when they deserve it, recognize and empathize with difficult times, and involve them in your planning, including goal setting, strategy, and problem solving.

Regarding compensation I will make only a few comments. Pay well, but with a portion of it in stock and bonuses so it is tied to both company and personal performance. The reason to pay well, and "well" means above average, is so that pay is not a nagging, demoralizing issue, and so that it is easy to hire whomever you choose.

Hold two- or three-day meetings of the entire marketing and sales organization, plus key people from the technical and manufacturing activities, at least once a year and preferably every six to eight months. The psychological "coming in from the cold," the actual informational exchange, and the team building possible from such gatherings more than pay the cost. At these meetings, acknowledge high performance resoundingly, both verbally and with tangible appropriate perks.

How to Motivate the Company Behind the Program

Against the deluge of writings on motivation, this section is not intended to be competition. Rather it is to plead for one certain motivational activity–arguably the most powerful of all.

The motivational tool I wish to lobby for with all the fervor and intensity I can is *involvement with the customer.* There is nothing that so compels the production manager to ship on Friday as the direct plea by the customer. There is nothing so stimulating to the creativity of the engineer as the customer asking personally, "Do you suppose you could develop something that would do this?" And that engineer, caught in the spirit of the moment, responding, "Yes, I think I can!"

As marketing or sales person it is *your* responsibility to be sure this contact happens. On sales calls to key customers, frequently bring along someone from another department who is vitally involved. When customers visit the plant, invite the involved people from all departments to be present and participate in the meeting. Instead of speaking for them, let them voice their own commitments to the customer. At lunch time, bring along someone from finance as well as R&D. On the tour of the plant, introduce the customer by name to the workers involved on the project. Explain your philosophy that as many of your people as possible should know the customer. The customer will appreciate this.

Your literature and advertising writers should have as much exposure as possible so they too can know "the story."

If this practice is followed, you will find that when the people in production, engineering, and so on know 10% of your key customers, it gives them a frame of reference for the others, and that spirit carries over to the other 90%.

This leads to the discussion of a special organizational alternative that may be desirable for bringing major new products to market, particularly in the setting of a larger company. It leverages off the principle of involvement with the customer.

The New Product Task Group

Traditionally, in a large ongoing company, a new product idea is developed in engineering, with or without any marketing input, then is "handed over" to manufacturing. Once manufacturability is established and an initial production run is underway it is "handed over" to marketing to sell. This process is loaded with booby traps, and even if none explodes, the time to get the product to market is unnecessarily long. Among the traps are: that the product is not designed to meet customer needs, that it is not economically manufacturable, that it will not be delivered to coincide with the marketing effort, and finally that everyone will be blaming everyone else for the problems.

One solution is a *new product task group* made up of the key marketing, engineering, and manufacturing people concerned with that product. They *all* are responsible for all phases being correct from the start. The very first step the group undertakes is to understand fully the market and product requirements. While the marketing person on the team is primarily responsible for this phase, the engineering and manufacturing people are actively involved, making calls and analyzing the information. This phase is done thoroughly and intensely but quickly at the beginning of the project, with customer requirements as the starting point of the design. With everyone on the team hearing the same customer input and sharing responsibility for the entire project, the timing of the marketing plan is continuously phased with both design and production plans.

The group leader, who must be a fanatic for the product and possess the most powerful and inspiring dream of anyone involved, must be responsible and have the authority to orchestrate the resources, even if some of the team members are only on assignment to the task and are still working for other bosses.

In short, this organizational concept utilizes customer-inspired motivation to its fullest while paralleling the activity of the engineering, manufacturing, and marketing functions.

Realistically, such a team cannot be established around every new product if your company is one that continuously introduces many new product variations. It can and should be done around major new ventures, particularly if new markets or new technologies are involved. With programs that are too frequent and too small to justify a task group the product "entrepreneur" can still accomplish nearly the same result informally. Here the product champion conducts a quick study of the market, involving the manufacturing and technical people informally. Then, as the project progresses, even though these people remain in different functions, they should continue to meet frequently.

A very important factor affecting the motivation of people during new product development must be emphasized here. That is, the road is rocky and fraught with discouragements. If everyone realizes this ahead of time, and keeps the customer-induced vision clearly in view, they can proceed much more smoothly than if they are isolated from the customer and from other functional activities of the program. This roller coaster ride from product inception to the sale has been cleverly and humorously (but very realistically) portrayed in the following graph by Mr. Bob Saldich, now President of Raychem Corporation, and is based upon his years of wisely guiding many new product ventures to success.

Your Plan

1. Chart the organization necessary to make your product go. Note the qualifications for each key person to see if all bases are covered.
2. Note where you best position yourself to maximize your joy and contribution.
3. What do you need right now to better motivate you regarding this product?
4. What do you need to do to better motivate others on the team?

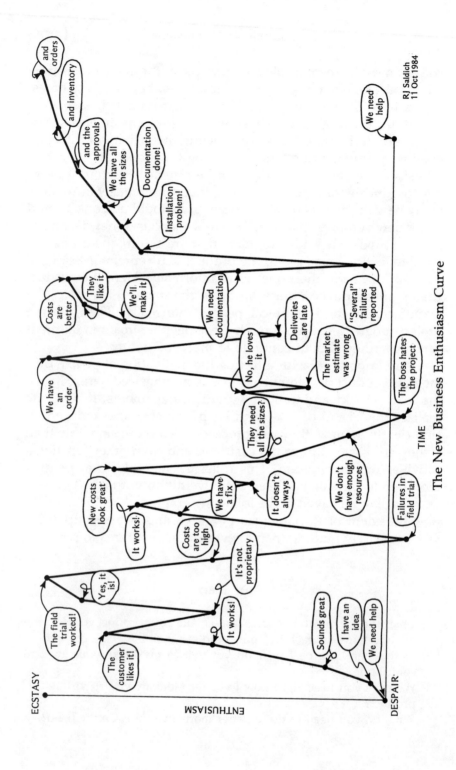

The New Business Enthusiasm Curve

RJ Saldich
11 Oct 1984

Knowing If It Will Work and If It Is Continuing to Work

T his chapter discusses the final phase of the marketing plan—its critical review. Quantitively, does it meet the financial goals, or is it financially optimized? Qualitatively, does it fulfill your values?

Quantitative Considerations

Now it is time to fit your dream of conquering that beckoning market with the costs of actually doing it. You have analyzed its size, set goals, decided on a strategy, and turned this into a proper marketing mix. Will it meet the financial targets you established in your goal? Let us view a simplified situation that illustrates the principles of goal setting and strategy planning outlined in Chapter 6.

Jasper Phardelton, Jr., Product Manger of the entrepreneurial spirit, was writing his business plan for the new automatic farbistrator his company, Xyzonitronics Inc., had developed. It was in a market totally separate from the rest of the company's business, so he had a "clean slate" as far as a marketing plan was concerned. It represented a diversification for the business, whose main activity was steam boilers. Farbistrators were used primarily in the chemical industry, and according to the industry association, The National Council of Farbistration, the market in 1989 was $165 million, with a historical and projected growth rate of 15% compounded annually. An industry survey by Burplebutte and Spitterspoon Associates, a market research firm, showed 1989 sales of $143 million and a growth rate of 12%. Jasper had surveyed the 15 leading customers personally and phoned an additional 20, and out of this extrapolated $150 million per year. He chose to go with a conservative $140 mil and set a target of capturing 1% during the first year, 4% the second, and 8% the third, since his product was better than the two major competitors in the field. Within seven years he hoped to have 20% of the then much larger market.

Fifty percent of the potential was among 40 customers located in six metropolitan regions. His data gathering led him to the very rough conclusion that an average of 10 sales calls would have a .50 probability of selling an account.

His "first cut" on a plan was to put six direct sales people in the field immediately. Advertising, trade shows, and the like would also be heavily utilized. These and his other assumptions are shown on Plan A.

Jasper was pleased with himself as he took his plan to Herman Haulke, the vice president of marketing who had built a reputation by launching several successful products. He was a portly man, with large flapping jowls that turned red and quivered when he got angry (which recently he had been doing frequently) but were milk-white and only jiggled when he hee-hawed. Jasper's pleasure stopped short when he saw it was a red quiver day. Herman glanced at the plan and threw it back at Jasper, saying he could spend only half that to get the program started. Jasper returned to his desk, angry and dejected. In fact, there was a slight quiver in his own round cheeks—but fortunately no one was there to see it.

However, Jasper was very conscientious and wanted desperately to be Marketing Vice President someday; so, after going to the bathroom, he went to his desk and recast the program much against his entrepreneurial instincts. He cut direct sales people to three, substituting reps in the lesser areas. He also cut promotion, and as a consequence of all this reduced the sales forecast. (see Plan B.) He was not quite to half, but if Herman had returned to a good mood he would probably agree.

Herman had left for the day by the time Jasper had finished, so he had to wait until the following day. However, at 4:45 Jasper got a call from a friend who worked for one of the potential customers saying a competitor was discussing a new farbistrator of comparable performance to be introduced about the same time as Jasper's.

The next morning Herman was in a jolly jiggle jowl mood, which pleased Jasper as he presented the plan. Herman liked it, until Jasper mentioned the competition. Herman's jowls suddenly blew out sideways—something Jasper had never seen before—and his whole face turned red as he shouted, "Fire the torpedoes!" (Herman's hobby was reading Naval history.) "Blast them, I don't care what it costs—blast them!" Jasper, in his cool analytical way, interpreted this to mean he could now implement a very aggressive strategy to gain market share before the competition introduced its product. (See Plan C.) (Later he was to learn Herman had been fired at the tender age of 23 by the man who was now president of the competitive firm.)

Thus, Plan C opted for market share (and satisfying Herman's unconscious) rather then shorter term profits. The final step in preparing the marketing plan is to fit it to a projected profit and loss test. Do the growth and profit figures meet your goal, keep the company healthy and investors happy? If not, go back to your computer spread sheet and do "what if" testing, much as Jasper did, to best meet your criteria.

Once you have a plan you feel comfortable with, at least every three months compare your projection to what has actually happened and review the remaining forecast, based upon what you have additionally learned.

Qualitative Considerations

If quantitative issues are being met, it is still extremely important for long-term success to answer most of the following questions positively.

- Are you making products you feel are worthwhile?
- Are these outstanding products being shipped on time, and functioning to the resounding joy of your customers?
- Do the customers seem like friends? Are they candid with you and you with them?
- Are you aware of your customers' next generation of needs?
- Do the customers suggest opportunities for you just outside your mainstream product line?
- Is your turnover of employees negligible?
- Do most of the outstandingly talented people to whom you offer jobs accept them?
- Is there a task-oriented team spirit among your employees?
- Will your marketing vice president still enthusiastically pack and ship that sample at 9:00 P.M.
- Are you proud of your company and the job you are doing in it?

In Non-Conclusion

I implied in the introduction that one should start a book without fanfare and I likewise believe one should stop without straining for a climax. However, in this case the book does not have an ending. It is simply one trip through the marketing cycle, and since the world has changed since you started reading it, you should go back to Chapter 4 and start again understanding your market.

Plan A

Marketing Mix (P&L)
$(000) Year

	1	2	3
Sales Projection (Level IV)	1,400	5,600	11,200
Cost of goods sold	1,000	3,300	6,000
Gross Margin	400	2300	5200
Expenses (1st yr basis)			
R&D 2 eng. & 2 tech.	300	400	800
G&A Corp. allocation 6%	84	336	672
Marketing			
Sales start w/6 direct; 4 more by 3rd yr	600	800	1,000
Distributors		not used	
Service start w/1 field srvc. engineer	100	200	5200
Literature			
Brochures 6 pg. 3 color	8	8	12
Specifications 2 pg. black/white	2	2	4
Test report 6 pg. black/white	4	4	6
Application data 6 pg. black/white	4	4	6
Case histories		2	4
Advertising 3 publ. 1 pg. 12 issues	85	85	85
Trade shows 2 ea. yr.	20	20	40
Seminars 6 regional	12	12	18
Publicity 4/yr. 5 publ.	2	2	2
Total marketing expense	837	1,139	1,477
Total expense	1,221	1,875	2,949
Profit before taxes	**(821)**	**425**	**2,251**

NOTE: 2nd and 3rd yr. expenses reflect estimated scale.

Plan B

Marketing Mix (P&L)
$(000) Year

	1	2	3
Sales projection (Level IV)	1,100	4,000	8,00
Cost of goods sold	800	2,400	4,300
Gross Margin	300	1,600	3,700
Expenses			
R&D	300	400	600
G&A	66	240	480
Marketing			
Sales 3 direct	300	400	500
Rep commission	17	60	120
(5% on 30% Sales)			
Distributors		not used	
Service	100	200	300
Literature			
Brochures	8	8	10
Specifications	2	2	3
Test reports	4	4	5
Application data	4	4	5
Case histories		2	4
Advertising 3 publ. 1 pg. 6	40	60	60
issues			
Trade shows	20	20	30
Seminars	12	12	18
Publicity	2	2	2
Total marketing expense	509	774	1,057
Total expense	875	1,414	2,137
Profit before taxes	**(575)**	**186**	**1,563**

Plan C

Marketing Mix (P&L)
$(000) Year

	1	2	3
Sales projection	1,600	7,000	12,000
Cost of goods sold	1,100	4,000	6,400
Gross margin	500	3,000	5,600
Expenses			
R&D	300	400	800
G&A	96	360	720
Marketing			
Sales 6+2 at mid year	700	1000	1,200
Rep commission 5% on 20% sales	16	60	120
Distributors	—	not used	—
Service 2 field srvc. engineer	200	300	400
Literature			
Brochures	8	8	12
Specifications	2	2	4
Test reports	4	4	6
Application data	4	4	6
Case histories		2	4
Advertising 3 publ. 1 pg. 9 issues	70	70	70
Trade shows	20	20	40
Seminars	12	12	18
Publicity	2	2	2
Total marketing expense	1,038	1,484	1,882
Total expense	1,434	2,244	3,402
Profit before taxes	**(934)**	**756**	**2,198**

Index

About the Author

Paul Sherlock brings to this book over twenty-five years of "practicing what he is preaching." He has spent much of his career with Raychem Corporation, where he brought to market a number of highly successful product lines and is now Director of Strategic Marketing for Corporate Technology.

He interrupted his Raychem career for twelve years during which he consulted and worked with start-up companies and then founded and was president of Kelsar Corporation, a medical plastics manufacturing company now owned by a major U.S. medical products firm.

Sherlock has pioneered, managed, or market researched a wide range of products, including electronic interconnections, solenoid actuators, medical plastics and instruments, medical computers, custom plastic fabrication, toys, hobby products, video equipment, chemical separation technology, plastic optics, local area networks, and fiber optics.

In addition, he has held executive positions or been on the board of directors of several high-technology companies.

Sherlock holds several patents in electrical interconnections, medical products, and optics.

He taught industrial marketing at Stanford University for two years and holds a B.S. in Mechanical Engineering from the University of Vermont, an M.S. in Psychology from Pacific Graduate School of Psychology, and an M.B.A. from Harvard University.